Secrets of Micro Publishing

For Those Who Aspire to Publish

Katie Isbester, Ph.D.

Copyright © Katie Isbester, 2025
The moral right of the author has been asserted.

ISBN paperback: 978-1-910461-78-5
ISBN ebook: 978-1-910461-79-2

All rights reserved. No part of this publication may be reproduced, stored in or introduced into a retrieval system, transmitted, in any form, or by any means (electronic, mechanical, photocopying, recording or otherwise) without the prior written consent of the publisher. Any person who does any unauthorised act in relation to this publication may be liable to criminal prosecution and civil claims for damages.

A CIP catalogue record for this book is available from the British Library.

This paperback can be ordered from all bookstores as well as from Amazon, and the ebook is available on online platforms such as Amazon and iBooks.

Cover and Interior Design by Petya Tsankova

www.claretpress.com

Table of Contents

Introduction	1
Part 1: Aspire	5
Part 2: Act	41
Part 3: Account	71
Part 4: Assess	95
Part 5: Announce	123
Part 6: Advance	147
Finally	165

Introduction:
Why This Book and What Will You Get From It

Why Did I Write This Book?
It had long bothered me that many of the excellent manuscripts I'd edited over the decades never found a publisher but languished instead in a bottom drawer. It struck me as a terrible shame. So I decided to do something about it. Not coincidentally, I was grappling with cancer at the time and needed something positive in my life. I needed to make something right.

Perhaps this is not the best reason to start a publishing company.

The past eight years have been a learning curve with considerable frustration, many dead ends and the occasional stunning success. Learning how to be a publisher has been jaw-droppingly inefficient.

I want to make it clear that I'd spent an awful lot of time on the internet researching how to be a publisher. I'd done my due diligence.

Yet, I learned that what worked for small publishers (that were nonetheless larger than I was) didn't work for me. Typically, small publishers had access to skilled workers, agents and distributors. They had access to funding and economies to scale. I didn't.

Self-publishers were a different animal. Too frequently they operated without a filter, and suggestions for improvement were beyond basic: get a proper cover, get it edited, tell a story, etc.

Occasionally I'd be in that long dark teatime of the soul and grumble: *Why is information for micro publishers not out there?*

So, I'm sharing what I know in the hope that all of you out there will have an easier ride of it. This guide lays out in simple terms how to go about the job of publishing at a very small scale.

What is a Micropublisher?

Micropublishing is publishing at so small a scale that it doesn't even qualify as a small business. To qualify as a small publisher in the UK you need to publish 12-15 titles a year and/or have an annual turnover of at least £50,000 ($70,000USD). It's similar in the USA and Canada. In a good year, I manage about five titles and have a turnover of around £10,000. I'm too small to be a small business. I'm micro.

In the USA and Canada, a micropublisher might be called an "indie". But the word indie has become meaningless. Any publisher that doesn't belong to the Big 5 is called an indie, and there is a rather large number of substantially sized indies. Bloomsbury (which published the Harry Potter series) was a medium-sized publishing company and now is strategically swallowing up small fry. But it's still an indie. Micropublishers have nothing in common with that kind of indie. Literally nothing.

So I'm not going to use the term "indie" or "small business".

Besides micro publishers like me, there are other kinds of micropublishing: a writer's group, where a clutch of authors gets together and publishes themselves under one umbrella; a college which has creative writing and/or art classes and wants to produce a few books a year to showcase their students' talents; and businesses for marketing purposes.

Many businesses publish a few titles a year to help to discreetly and organically promote their products. For example: glossy artbooks about wine from a vineyard; intriguing house designs from architects and interior designers; highly illustrated stories from a co-op of illustrators; non-fiction about overcoming adversity from a wellness NGO; the history of gems from a jeweller. There is no expectation that these books will make money. They're about showcasing and promoting and nudging.

> TRUE STORY: I edited and then helped the author to self-publish books. He had a PhD in mathematics from Imperial College, a post-doc from Harvard and worked as a consultant in the IT industry. According to him, too few people with a degree in data science truly understood the maths. So he set up a

little publishing company and produced a book of mathematics a year appropriate for mid-level professionals in the industry. While the books would undoubtedly help those in the industry, he was also raising his profile in the industry and promoting himself as an expert.

So this book of mine is helpful to all sorts of "publishers".

Equally, let me lay out clearly what this book is NOT. It is NOT how to write a murder mystery or a romance. It is NOT a book about how to adroitly use Kindle Select versus Kindle Direct Publishing (KDP). Or how to get likes on LinkedIn, TikTok or Instagram. It is NOT a guide to syntax, diction or editing mark-ups. Or how to use InDesign to create a PDF. There are loads of books, blogs, videos and podcasts available on those topics, some of which I've found to be useful.

This is – to the best of my knowledge – the only book on micropublishing. And I wrote it because there is a resounding silence about the specific needs of micropublishers.

I would go so far as to say that we have more in common with other tiny businesses than we do with even small publishers. I've had useful conversations with a man who started a travel agency, a fashion designer selling her own work, a couple who fix crumbling old iron fireplaces and an opera buff who created an opera company. These microproducers are encountering the same kinds of problems that I am, and we share useful tips about how to succeed.

Publishing is project management. It's the journey that a work takes from its creator to its buyer. Along the way, the micropublisher has to learn how to work with creators, be an accountant, oversee a project from beginning to end, learn new technology, market to a niche and strategise for development. And that's just for starters. It's challenging, to put it mildly. And fun. And deeply fulfilling.

If you're a micropublisher then this guide might offer information appropriate to your reality: terminology, processes, strategies. Throughout, I'll be telling you what I've done, honestly and openly. I'll share my successes and failures in the hope that you can build on the former and avoid the latter.

If you look at the Table of Contents, you'll see exactly what I am telling you: the big picture and the little, the money and the marketing, the organising and the fun. You might already know some of it. In which case, skip that chapter.

Step by step, this book will take you through the growth necessary to create a vibrant micropress based on your own goals and skills. Your micropress will not look like my micropress, Claret Press. It will instead be exactly the kind of publishing house that you want it to be. So this book is not an IKEA pictogram where we all end up with the same Billy bookcase. Instead, it assumes that you are thoughtful and can apply the knowledge to the specifics of your own situation.

My experience has been that people in publishing are the nicest group of people you'll ever meet. We are not each other's competition. The Big 5 and Netflix and video games are our competition, as is the sheer exhaustion at the end of our day. I hope that the readers of this book will gain something from it and become more efficient and effective publishers, producing and selling to an improved standard, with more joy and less frustration, greater success and fewer mistakes.

My best wishes to all of you.

Part 1: ASPIRE

You have to know what your goals are before you start or you won't know if you are achieving what you want to achieve. What you aim for tends to be what you get.

1A) Choose the Kind of Publisher You Want to Be

You know those diagrams of how an entire industry works: a pyramid with a vast number of small producers along the bottom and as the pyramid narrows, the number of companies decreases but their size increases. These are medium-sized businesses. At the pinnacle are the multinational corporations that bestride the world like behemoths.

So that's not publishing.

Instead, there is a massive number of itsy-bitsy micros in a thick wodge along the bottom and then the Big 5 at the pinnacle. There is precious little between the two layers.

If you plan on growing your company from a micro to a small to a medium-sized company, you have to take this reality into consideration.

If this all sounds grim, fear not. There is a mushrooming of multiple forms of small indies.

Now look, being commercially viable might not matter to you if you are part of a writing co-op, or you have a trust fund, or you can figure out how to get government funding. As I have none of that, I tend to sweat the pennies.

To that end, I have examined different forms of micropublishing. How you approach publishing is up to you, but if you are starting up a press or thinking of revamping your press, changing its shape and what it produces, you might be interested in these different forms.

1. **Aggregate Press**
   Aggregate publishing is a compromise between traditional publishing and self-publishing. Just as the name implies, an aggregate press collects up everything and publishes it. There is little to no filter. It doesn't edit or shape or promote. It may or may not put a cover on the book.

The largest in the world is Smashwords in the USA. They only do ebooks, which they usually upload to Amazon. Covers are AI-generated or standard. These aggregate publishers might also act as their own platforms for the reader to download ebooks. They exist on the profit made from the sales once the costs, including royalties to the authors, have been paid. They charge the author no fee so technically it's not self-publishing but legit publishing. I once read in an article that these aggregates make £1 on every download. The assumption is that every author will sell between 100 and 250 copies of their own book to friends and family, which more than covers the costs of that book. If the occasional one sells more, then that's cream. Volume is key to its business model.

Personally, I don't see much of a future for aggregate presses, except for erotica or really niche reads (such as Google-Translated versions of Chinese-language kung-fu stories). Aggregate presses preceded Amazon and have now been eclipsed by Amazon. They are actively seeking authors because Amazon is putting them out of business.

2. **Hybrid Publishers**

Again, the name says it all. Hybrid presses combine aspects of both traditional publishing (where the publisher pays for the editing, cover design, distribution, marketing and then pays the author a % of the money that the title earns) and of self-publishing (where the author pays for everything). There are many different versions of hybrid publishing so it's hard to make a definitive statement about what they are in detail, but the key issue is that the author pays somehow at some point with the publisher paying other costs.

Examples are: The publishing company covers the costs but the author receives no royalties until the costs have been recovered (the costs are usually never recovered). The author pays for the editing and proofreading and the cover design, then the author and the publisher share royalties 50-50 (which pays for the publisher's associated costs like a website). The publisher pays for the ebook but the paperback is paid for by the author. Or the author has to buy 250 copies of the book (which covers the cost of producing the book and is likely what the author would sell anyway to family and friends). You can slice this and dice this all sorts of ways.

I think hybrid publishing is a reasonable way to go forward if you want to set up shop as a publisher and you don't have any capital to risk. As you become successful, you can start to take chances on authors who might not get you any royalties. Or if the author is poor and can't afford the whole cost of production, you can cut them some slack.

It offers authors the same quality and care that they get from a traditional publisher and considerably more control over the production process, as he who pays the piper calls the tune. It is for authors who can't get agents and therefore can't get a traditional publisher. And most debut authors can't.

Also it frankly acknowledges that no one is really going to make money out of publishing. Not the publisher and not the author. This is about reducing risk to the publisher's capital while offering an author what is needed to get the book professionally published.

Authors who have made their peace with this reality might appreciate working with a company that has a vested interest in producing and distributing a well written, well designed book. The bonus is that, if the author is discreet, no one need know that the author contributed to the cost of publication, so it avoids the stigma of self-publishing. Indeed, the author can do what every author everywhere does: complain about how pitifully small the royalty cheque is and how little marketing the publisher is doing for the book.

3. **Specialist ebook publishers**
These publishers tend to only be in a few genres: romance, crime and self-help/psychology. Crime and romance are the two genres that sell the most copies and the most new titles. People can read crime and romance almost obsessively, and even those who look you dead in the eye and claim they never read, will read crime and romance.

Prices for these ebooks tend to be cheaper but that's because it's a 'stack-em-high-sell-em-cheap' model. More importantly, the risk to capital is minimal. If no one buys the ebook, nothing has to be pulped. And really most people can create a digital book with the right piece of software and instruction. And keep in mind that the author will reasonably sell about 250 copies. The publisher can sell at least the same amount using modern marketing strategies, that is, data scraping. That tends to mean that more copies get sold. This is good. But there is a down side.

First, you really have to know your genre, the specifics of what sells strongly. The author can't stray too far from what the algorithm says will sell. As a result, a lot of the books seem as if they're written from a template. In effect, they have been.

Second, because they're solely ebooks, readers can't order them through their local bookshop so authors automatically lose a portion of their readers. Solely ebooks don't show up on any awards list. The authors simply don't get the standing that they might have otherwise acquired.

Third, what makes these ebook publishers commercially viable is that they truly understand how to manipulate algorithms, do funnel marketing and how to get a ROI when buying ads on Amazon and Facebook. Believe me when I say that these skills are marketed as easier to do and more lucrative than they actually are. I once spent £200 advertising a book on Amazon and sold one ebook, which I probably would have sold anyway. And it's not as if I hadn't put in the hours and done the workshops and read the how-to's.

I do, however, know a man who self-publishes crime thrillers as ebooks. He's been moderately successful. He uses exactly the same strategies to market his books as he does in his day job, where he markets women's hosiery through digital technology. So he already knew what he was doing. He is a skilled and experienced marketer.

If you know of anyone who already has these skills and wants to share them with you or is prepared to be paid in the form of royalties, then this might be a reasonable way to go forward.

Having said that, I found it truly depressing that of all the time this man spent on his books, a good half was spent marketing. So here was a highly experienced marketer, efficient and effective in a way that few are, and it still took him half of his precious free time to flog his books.

After he told me this, I had to go lie down.

4. *Traditional but at the micro level*
This is me. I have a hard time recommending it as I haven't yet made enough money to relax my husband. I'm getting there but I also think it's the nature of the beast of traditional publishing. Few, if any, ever get to the spot where we're rolling in. For a small indie, the definition of success is being bought out by Penguin Random House.

This is the way that we're traditional: we pay the authors, they don't pay us (see chapter on royalties). All costs are borne by us. We own the copyright to the work (see chapter on copyright). We take care of printing, warehousing and distributing the work (again, see all the appropriate chapters). Like the Big 5 we produce press releases (see chapter on marketing).

This is the way that we're not traditional: We care, generally far too much, and we spend a debilitating amount of time with each title. We edit, discuss, re-edit and edit again, proofread, design and upload the work. We hand-hold the authors, attend every book launch and get to know the authors' friends and family (if only because we sleep at their houses after the launch). We don't use agents or data mining engineers to tell us what will sell; we haven't got a clue about whether or not a book fits an algorithm. We seem to be less business-driven than other kinds of publishers, although I personally really wouldn't mind balancing the books.

I want to put a qualifier out. There are publishers that mix and match these four general types. They might be traditional but also have a hybrid arm. They might be traditional but also have an aggregate ebook arm. They might be hybrid and aggregate. They might be aggregate and yet cherry-pick the ones to push through their specialist ebook arm.

Myself, I have a paying arm. That is, I have two companies. One is Claret Press, which is my traditional micropress. However, I also continue to sell my editing services, have expanded to offer proofreading services and help authors to self-publish. I use the same book designer and editor and proofreader. I sometimes use the same printer. It helps to keep the people who work for me employed and that makes us all happy. So I am not criticising those who combine different types of publishing. You do what you can to survive in the creative industry.

1B) Choose the Journey You Want Your Books To Take

To choose the kind of publisher you want to be, it might help to understand how books are printed up and reach their readers. I'm going to sketch out that journey.

So first, the **traditional** model but at the micro level. So we're not talking about the Big 5 here. We're talking about you and me.

And here's why. With the Big 5, data mining engineers might choose the specifications of debut authors in conjunction with the marketing department. They inform the agents, who rifle through their authors until they find one that more or less fits the bill, then tweak the work until it's a better fit. Then it gets sent to the editors.

> TRUE STORY: Through my other company, Clapham Publishing Services, I edited for a fee a book that got accepted by a big American publisher. Whoo-hoo! I was slack-jawed to discover that the editor at this company only read the first three chapters before the contract was signed. Then the book got a line edit. Before the line edit was finished, the marketing department had changed the title, produced several covers, and been in contact with the author about what she intended to do to sell the book.

In other words, the marketing department was in at the first step, telling the editor to accept a manuscript because it fit some demographic slice. The editor decided it was well enough written based on the first few thousand words that they read, and sent out a contract.

If you are in business, this all seems very reasonable. If you are a creator, your toes are curling in horror.

Micropublishers, even specialist micropublishers, read every single word of every book that they produce, generally multiple times. While the micropublisher may talk to the author about how best to sell the book, almost certainly marketing does not lead. Maybe marketing should. That's probably why we're micros.

A final draft of the book is produced. It then gets sent off to a printer and copies get printed up. The printer then sends them to a distributor. The distributor has sales reps who pitch the title to libraries and bookshops. The pitch is based on the marketing material that the publisher has shared with the distributor. The bookshops order copies of the title from the distributor or wholesaler, and sell them to readers.

It's a long journey from the author writing the book to the reader buying it.

Let's add money into the equation. Some payments are up front and some payments are on consignment, which means that the publisher doesn't get any money until after the reader has bought the book at the very end of the journey.

All bookshops take books on consignment. This means that if your book doesn't sell then they can either send it back to the warehouse – on the publisher's penny – or toss it out, and if there are any costs associated with tossing it out then that's also on the publisher's penny. What they're not going to do is waste valuable shelf space on your book if it doesn't make the bookshop any money. If a customer browsing in the bookshop doesn't look at your book and say *oooh I like that, I'm going to buy that*, then your book will not last on the bookshelf for very long. The maximum time a title tends to spend on a bookshelf is several months. Those huge bookshops with multiple floors of books and a café use books as a kind of wallpaper. They might carry a title for as long as six months. Of course, if the title sells, then it stays.

Still on the topic of money: a bookshop can charge the recommended retail price (RRP) or more or less. Amazon uses books as a gateway drug. Its business model is based on selling books more cheaply than elsewhere. The reader then builds a trust relationship with the company and does more shopping on its platform. It sells below the RRP if the title is no longer moving and it wants to clear its warehouse.

The bookshop keeps a % of what the reader pays and then gives the remaining amount back to the distributor. The distributor then keeps a previously agreed upon % and returns the rest to the publisher. The % that the distributor keeps is negotiated. It depends on how many sales everyone thinks that there's going to be, the number of titles that the publisher has with that distributor, and so on. The distributor can keep as much as 65% of the RRP.

Then the publisher gives the author a % of each copy sold. And that % changes depending on where you are in the world. If you're from Continental Europe then you get a % of the RRP, but if you're English or American, then you get a % of the net return. And the reason for that is quite simple: Amazon. Continental Europe has protected itself against the depredations of Amazon and, as a result, the RRP is fixed. In the United States, Canada and the UK, Amazon has made a fixed RRP obsolete and can sell your books for substantially less than what the RRP has to be for the publishers to break even. Publishers have protected themselves by changing the rules of the game. In other words, they don't give any money back to the authors if it doesn't first arrive in their own bank accounts. Somebody has to pay for Amazon and the cost is being borne by authors.

Before the publisher gets back any money from the sale of the book through the bookshop, the publisher has already paid upfront for the editor, the proofreader, the designer and the marketer, among a host of other costs associated with being a publishing house. These people might be salaried but more typically they are on contracts. The publisher also has to pay upfront a fee to the printer, unless the publisher is producing print-on-demand.

So the publisher has invested highly in this book.

In a very traditional model, the publisher might give the author what's known as an advance, a certain amount of money which the author has to earn back through royalties. You have to be very sure of your marketing and how many books you're going to sell before you offer an advance. Because I'm a micropublisher and I work with first-time authors, I don't offer an advance. I have no idea how many books I'm going to sell; it's a mystery to me. So I pay my authors a % of the net receipts of the RRP after the money is paid to me. As publishing becomes more uncertain, fewer advances are given out, even by the Big 5. Celebrities still get them. Franchise authors get them. People who have an enormous social media following get them. That's about it.

You can play with that traditional model if you're a micropublisher or a self-publisher. You can bypass the editor, proofreader and marketer and go directly from the manuscript to the printer. And then it's possible, although such a pain in the neck, such a palaver, to get it into the warehouse at the big bookshops, or with a distributor. Some distributors are set up to deal with micropublishers or self-publishers. It is possible, although not easy or efficient or even reasonable, for the micropublisher to get their books into a wholesaler, which can then send them to bookshops. Besides the huge amount of work, there's nothing saying that the warehouse will actually put the book on the shelf of the bookshop so that it can be "discovered" by the reader. In fact, unless there is a superior marketing plan that guarantees sizeable number of sales, it's unlikely that bookshops will ever put a book distributed like this on their shelves.

So I don't recommend that micropublishers or self-publishers do this because of the high level of risk involved. All this work gets done, all this capital is risked on printing up copies, and the book still doesn't get into the bookshops.

Here's the big conclusion: the infrastructure of traditional publishing doesn't want to deal with micropublishers. It's polite but you can't miss the message. Personally, I think this whole process is nuts. Traditional publishing is a 19th century business model that has grown and grown until it's become unwieldy and overly complicated. It exists through sheer inertia. Everyone has already bought into this system and by gum they're not going to change it. This made it low-hanging fruit for the digital economy. When Amazon started in 2000, there were — believe it or not — those in the publishing industry who quietly celebrated it as they foresaw a modernisation of the industry. This was before everyone realised how predatory Amazon was.

Here are some examples of micropublishers who have gotten around that reality.

If you have a strong subscription service where you know you'll be able to sell your books guaranteed to your own people, then you can print up books in advance and put them in a warehouse. Then the role of the bookshop becomes of less importance. It's more the icing on the cake. If you tie your books into events like a rock concert, an organic food fair or an exhibit at a museum, then you can reasonably be assured of a certain number of sales. Again, you print those up in advance, put them in a warehouse and sell them.

Obviously, if you publish art books or books where the visuals are important, like children's literature or books intended for a certain kind of reader (the traveller, say) then you'll want them in a specialist bookshop. And again, a distributor is useful for that.

> TRUE STORY: I know a retired professor of music history who publishes books on, yes you guessed it, music history. He does about five books a year, if not fewer. He's a micropublisher. The books are hard cover. They're glossy. They're expensive. His wife does the editing and book design. He prints up 250 copies, which are sold to libraries throughout the world and to specialist music bookshops. He uses the university's publishing house's distributor and warehouse. They are part of the university's publishing newsletter that is sent out to bookshops and libraries. He always sells out. And once all the copies are sold, they're sold. That's it. He doesn't print up more because it's too high risk.
>
> He makes money off his micropress, and you can see why. All his ducks are lined up: the narrow brand so that people recognise what he is selling; the target audience with deep pockets; the warehousing and distribution; the cost of editing and designing go to his wife; the people who write the books are undoubtedly academics who get 2% royalties and if they don't make a dime, they won't complain.

So it's entirely possible as a micropress to be the traditional model and be successful.

Let's talk about the **print-on-demand** model, the digital model, where you only print one book at a time. In my opinion this makes a whole lot of sense, especially when you're just starting out.

With print-on-demand, you still have a manuscript. You still are the publisher. You still have all the work that you do with the manuscript in terms of editing and proofreading and designing and marketing. But the printer, distributor, warehouse, wholesaler, that all becomes one step: print-on-demand.

The first step is the same. The author creates a book. As a micropublisher you upload it to the print-on-demand platform which is, through the magic of the internet, available to every bookshop and individual. When someone goes into a shop to buy it, the print-on-demand company sends it to the bookshop. And that bookshop could be on the high street or an eplatform like Amazon, it could be here or in some other country. In theory, the bookshop could have it in a few days. At the moment, it takes longer.

This reduces upfront costs for the micropublisher. As a result, the risk for the micropublisher is lower. You're not paying a printer up front. If the book sells, you're not giving the distributor 65% of the RRP; you're giving the bookshop 35-40% of the RRP. If the book doesn't sell then you're not paying for pulping your book. You're not caught in that terrible cash flow squeeze that the traditional model asks out of publishers. Plus you get the long tail.

The long tail is one of the advantages of the internet and it means you endlessly sell the same title but not very often. Think of sales as being a cat. The bulk of the sales are the body of the cat and they will happen within 6-24 months. Then the sales peter out and become fewer and fewer. Every year you continue to sell a copy or two. For your lifetime. This is the long tail. It won't make you much money but it does make you feel good about yourself. And that's not nothing. The long tail happens because the book is stored as a PDF in the cloud and downloaded, printed up, distributed and sold as requested.

> TRUE STORY: The first book I ever published was written by the auntie of a friend. She was a retired British Museum worker who also taught evening courses at Birkbeck College. She'd written a number of well-regarded books on Ancient Egypt. She took her considerable knowledge of the classics and turned it into a kiddie book: *Stories from Herodotus*. I got it illustrated. I uploaded it to print-on-demand. I sell two dozen copies a year every year to aspirational parents around the world. It just sits there up on the internet as print-on-demand and I'll probably still be selling it on my deathbed. Eventually all those sales will ensure that it breaks even. I doubt it will ever do more.

Print-on-demand also makes your accounting easier. Deducted at source is the cost of printing that copy, the cost of distributing it and the cost kept by the bookshop. You get one spreadsheet with how many copies were sold of a title and the final amount deposited into your account.

If you want to figure out your profit at the end of the financial year, you subtract from the money deposited in your bank account, the author's royalty and the fixed costs (the amount you spent on the upload, the book designer and any incidentals). What's left is profit. That's practically no maths at all.

The disadvantage of this model is that you have to make sure that your marketing is targeted at the reader, because the system is exactly as its name says it is: demand-driven. In theory, if enough people ask for this title from their bookshops then the wholesaler and Amazon start to stock it and bookshops are more inclined to stock it if you nudge them. If you create the demand then the supply takes care of itself.

But marketing is always tricky.

I publish both through print-on-demand and through a traditional distributor. I do print-on-demand for areas where I can't get a distributor, that is Canada, the USA and Australia. I have a traditional distributor for the UK and EU.

I hope this simple overview has helped you to decide which kind of publishing journey you want your books to go on.

1C) Four Issues to Consider Before You Start

There is much to be said for sealing your doubts in a lead-lined box, locking it and tucking it under your bed.

And yet...

Before you start, you might want to consider a few things. And these things are not the nuts and bolts of micropublishing, but something deeper, something specific to just you and to no one else. Indeed, there is no right or wrong answer. You can change your answers as you get more experienced. You don't have to tell anyone your thought processes or the answers. There's no need to write them up as a blog or share them on Instagram. If you feel the desperate need to talk this one out, I recommend getting a dog.

Here are some issues to consider before you start.

The first is about **goals.** What are you truly going for? If you need to, make a list with the most important goals at the top and then go on down to the trivial. Once you have done that, you will know what kind of a publisher you are going to be and loads of other decisions fall into place.

Let's look at some options.

You might be at the point in your life where what you want is just to get yourself and your mates published and have a bit of a lark. It's a great way to see your words in print. You aren't going to get your knickers in a twist about proofreading or money or deadlines. This is a way of scratching that writing itch while keeping it fun, making friends and learning a lot. If so, then structure your publishing around that.

Conversely, you might be young and funky, hip and happening, and want to use your books to promote a broader creative endeavour, get a job or just upset the apple cart. The way that you publish will reflect those goals.

As for myself, I want to publish the kind of books that mean something to me. If I don't love the manuscript to bits, then I don't publish it. I am personally involved in everything I publish.

This means that I have control over the book I'm publishing. I'm the ultimate decision maker. Not the marketing team. Not the bank manager. And if it doesn't sell, well, let the chips fall where they may.

> TRUE STORY: *Dangerous Skies* by Brian James is based on the author's own life. It's about growing up during the Blitz here in South London. It's war seen from a child's perspective. It's terrifying, enraging, heartwarming and completely non-nostalgic. Nigel Farage would hate it. It's got original artwork and a fabulous design. The author, who is obviously now in his 80s, loves it. And the kids who have read it, love it. Most importantly, I love it. It's the kind of book I would have loved at the age of 10, and the kind of book I would have liked to have read to my children. The problem is that *Dangerous Skies* doesn't fit my publishing brand. To which I say, *too bad*. I have perhaps said those two words a little too often to be successful.

It was also important to me to have flexibility in my schedule so that I could look after my aging mother and my excitable teenagers. I'm being pulled in two generational directions so I'm willing to put a premium on flexibility.

What was a more minor concern is money because I make my money from being paid to edit people's books through my companion company, Clapham Publishing Services. I have been a freelance editor for years and that brings in some cash.

Preference and flexibility. I've structured my publishing company around those two poles. They're my yin and my yang.

Because of my emphasis on these two values, I will realistically never be a wealthy publisher. Or even break even. That's the price I pay for my goals.

Make your peace with your own goals.

Find your own North and South Poles, your salt and pepper, the lace in your shoe. Once you've done that, you'll discover what kind of publisher you're going to be.

Having said what I just said about money being less important relative to flexibility and being able to control which books I publish, let's now talk about **money**. It's an awkward topic but let's do it anyway.

There is a lot of romance about the idea of publishing. Authors are romantics, and so are publishers. You almost have to be in order to invest so much with little expectation of a return. Instead, we indulge in romantic fantasies.

So let me tell you how the fantasy goes: you publish something fabulous and the world celebrates your extraordinary wisdom in choosing this author and, in the process, makes you rich and famous. And then because we're all mature adults and you know that won't happen, you dial it down to something merely impressive.

And then something merely impressive never happens. Even after you've put in a punishing amount of work. I'm really sorry about that. Truly.

To confuse matters, this fantasy does occasionally come true. A mid-sized indie called Bloomsbury published an unknown author called J.K. Rowling, and it made everyone involved in any aspect of Harry Potter, any aspect at all, rich. Or at least less poor. So it does happen.

Having said that, if that's your game plan, if that's how you intend to retire with a well-feathered nest, then buy lottery tickets instead.

As the joke goes: How do you make a small fortune in publishing? First you start off with a large fortune...

Publishing is a labour of love more than anything else, especially micropublishing. Authors are cranky with you for not selling more books and getting them on TV. Distributors don't want to know your name. Your lawyer replies to your queries with single word responses. (This truly happened to me. He once wrote in response to a query, *Yes*. In fairness, he also didn't charge me for the time he spent writing that.) Everyone thinks we're quixotic fools. And indeed we are.

So here's the awkward question you have to ask yourself: can you afford to be a micropublisher?

As I came out of cancer, still quite sick but well enough to wonder if I should continue this romantic quixotic foolish notion of publishing books, my husband said to me: *Make yourself happy; we'll survive*. He's the kind of man who says what he means and means what he says. So I did. And I *am* happy doing this. And I *am* glad that I tilt at windmills. But financially it was really really *really* dumb. So if you're not absolutely confident of your ability to afford being a micropublisher, then you might want to reconsider.

Here's something that you really have to recognise before you start, and that's the dominance of **technology**.

There's been a digital revolution. People now read on a Kindle, their phone, an iPad or listen to an audiobook. The physical construct of a book has changed, and as a result so has publishing.

Here's how we benefit from it as micropublishers. First and most obviously, the digital revolution modernised the book trade and permitted micropublishers like us to exist. We can print-on-demand so our risk is reduced. We can publish only in certain formats like ebooks or audio. We can publish from our laptops on the kitchen table or sitting in bed in our pyjamas. This ease of publishing was unknown in previous generations.

The digital revolution also permits us to do the marketing to sell our books, or to at least tell the world about our books through social media. Again, laptop. Pyjamas. Kitchen table.

I have now been a micropublisher for eight years and when people ask me what I have learned the most from the experience, I say technology.

Here's why you need to get on top of technology. Technology permits your micropress to work efficiently and effectively. The whole point of the digital (originally known as electronic) revolution is that your computer does the work, you don't. A micropublisher is an e(lectronic) business. You don't need to hire many people, or indeed anyone, because your computer does all the work with the press of the button.

But you've got to know which button to press.

Let me give you an example. I used to print out pieces of paper with graphs and numbers on them, which I then collated and filed in large ring binders. Then my son, who is studying engineering, wrote me a bookkeeping programme, bespoke, so that I just drag and drop all the Excel spreadsheets sent to me from the bank or distributor or whomever and the computer crunches the numbers. It takes literally a few minutes once a month, from opening the emails to closing them down, to do that month's bookkeeping. And about the same amount of time to figure out the royalties I owe my authors.

I can't even make myself a cup of tea in that time. That kind of efficiency should be considered as precious to you as hen's teeth.

In truth, I still prefer paper.

The best way I can think of technology is as a foreign language. You have to make the commitment to learn it, knowing that it's going to take a while, you're going to make mistakes and you're not going to understand what people are saying to you. It's going to be frustrating and hard work. Certainly, you'll never be as fully conversant as a native speaker. That's me with technology.

If you can, make your peace with that reality. If you can't or won't learn the technology then you have to rethink how you intend to be a micro-publisher.

And finally, something to consider: Who do you plan on **selling** to? Face to face, to family and friends, through your church group or summer fair, bridge club or footie group? From your website? Are you a natural salesperson? That is, can you sell well or are you shy and hesitant in a group?

And how do you plan on selling? Cash? Trade it for a beer or three? Credit cards? Or maybe you don't really plan on selling it anyway. It's for your family and friends.

The people you plan on selling your books to will shape the kind of books you choose to print, and how you structure your micropublishing company.

Here's why this is important. Micropublishers have close relationships with their authors. Part of the package is that, as a publisher, you can get them things that a self-publisher cannot. Like distribution. Like a good-looking appropriate cover. Like readers. Maybe not a lot of readers but some at least.

The digital revolution and social media have permitted books to get published to each tiny slice of the population who are interested in that one topic. They might be interested in the park benches of South London. You might find that amusing but don't laugh. If you can find the audience, then you can sell a book to them. This is a viable business model and proving successful. So narrow down your demographic to its tiniest sliver. Epic poetry about sailing. Stick man cartoons about maths. Translations of Eastern European 19th-century Jewish classics. By the way, all those examples are genuine and successful micropublishers.

To recap: the four issues to consider:

1. What are your goals?
2. Can you afford to be a micropublisher?
3. Are you prepared to get on top of the technology?
4. Who do you plan to sell to?

In a way, if you've answered the first question — what your goals are — then you've answered all four. The other three are almost other ways of asking the same question as the first: what's your goal?

Sit on this question for a long time. Be really honest with yourself.

Because I was quite sick when I started, my first authors understood that I might not be around to finish the job. Why they stuck with me is beyond me, but bless them, they did. My goal then was simply to finish the job. Get those books out to a high quality that we could all be proud of. It was such a simple goal.

That's no longer my goal. My goal (singular) has become my goals (plural). My ambitions are now more complex and fuzzier. Boundaries are not so clearly defined, more like lines drawn on a beach. I revisit these fuzzy goals on a regular basis. It's necessary.

1D) Three Things You Need Before You Start

When I started publishing, I wanted to do everything right. I researched and took notes and did what I was told to do. Some things I discovered were necessary, the occasional one wasn't. It's just so much easier to do things in the right order. So you do these things first:

1. *Get a Company*
   If you're living in the UK and you publish at any level, including self-publishing, I would recommend you turn your published works into a company.

   There are psychological reasons.

   As a micropublisher — meaning that you are publishing other people's books — you are a genuine publisher. The legal structure of your publishing company should reflect that reality. It's a signal that tells your authors and your readers that you are professional and committed and legal.

   You are what you say you are. You may only publish a couple of books a year, but you take it seriously enough to get the appropriate legal framework for a publishing house.

   Besides those psychological aspects, there are pragmatic reasons why you should create a publishing company:

   - People can look your publishing company up in Companies House and that might mean that they'll send you their manuscripts. You might not want their manuscripts but that's a different issue.
   - When you put books up for awards, the committee can research your company to decide whether or not to accept your submission. If you're self-published and you have no company, the committee might not accept your submission. And then your potentially award-winning book won't even be in the running.

- If you're part of a writing group or a writing co-op or a creative writing class, the legal framework helps to resolve issues before they arise. In the same way that good fences make good neighbours, a simple but clear legal framework for the publishing company makes it clear what everyone has signed up to.

It's dead easy to set up a company through Companies House here in the UK, and it doesn't cost much. It's also relatively simple to end it, assuming that you haven't gone into debt. If there's debt then it gets more complicated. But debt's like that.

The next question is, what kind of company should you be? Should you be a sole trader or have a limited liability partnership. There's a ton of information about it on the internet and I suggest that you go through it and see what works best for you. The kind of micro-publisher you are, the kind of books you publish, the number of people involved in your projects and the arrangements you make with your authors will determine which kind of company you want to have.

I suggest an LLP, the limited liability partnership, because you get a limited protection from loss in the event of things going wrong financially. The only thing that you can lose is your company's assets, not your house or other savings.

Let's say you get accused of libel and defamation. Not defaming or libelling someone in the first place is a better strategy to avoid being sued. But should the unexpected happen, being an LLP is a stronger legal position and you're a little better protected from being sued.

Let's say an author is cranky about (choose as appropriate) typos/sales numbers/cover design/editing/publication date/whatever and takes you to court. You lose. The cranky author gets your laptop and any other assets that the company owns (namely the copyrights to all the books that you've published). The cranky author is now the publisher. You don't even pay the legal fees because the author has sued your LLP, not you, and your LLP doesn't have any assets to sell to pay your lawyers. All you can do is wash your hands of the whole fandangle, take a recuperative trip to Tuscany and let the cranky author sort it all out.

An LLP also protects you if you go bankrupt. Let's say you print up 2,000 copies of a title, thinking that it'll sell like hotcakes. It doesn't. They sit in a warehouse or under your desk. Eventually they need to be pulped. You haven't yet paid your book designer or illustrator. You come to the slow realisation that this book won't sell. And you have no assets (besides copyrights and your old laptop). You declare bankruptcy. Technically you don't have to pay your creditors.

Look, it's all more complicated than I just told you. Words like debt structuring, HMRC and insolvency crop up. These are words that can keep a person awake at night. The point is that the LLP is a mode of protecting your stuff (house, retirement savings, grandma's furniture) so that you lessen the risk of bad things happening to you when you set up a business. If you're running a micropress, then it's good protection.

The last word of an LLP is partnership. The partner could be your best friend or your mother. My business partner is my husband, who hasn't a clue about what I'm doing or why. He's a great partner to have, in every meaning of the word.

A way that some publishers start out (especially if they are publishing themselves and their friends) is as a sole trader. For this, you don't need a partner. You can use your personal bank account and you do not need to have a business bank account.

In comparison, if your press is an LLP, then you need to have a business bank account. I have a business account with Santander, which was recommended as the best bank for small businesses. I have no complaint with it. But it's also charging me around £10 a month for the privilege of putting my money in its bank. And for the life of me, I don't see what I'm getting for that £120 a year that I don't get for free with my personal account. And nobody knows that I have a Santander business account rather than a Santander personal account. So this gets me nothing in the eyes of the rest of the world and in my own eyes as well. But it's the law so I do it.

2. **Get a Website**

   The second thing you should have **before you start** is have a website. A website is a modern-day business card. It used to be that you'd whip out a business card and pass it out at various events. I have business cards but gosh it's tough to get rid of them. Now, when you meet someone, you tell them the name of your website. Or show it to them on your phone. Or text them the link or a QR code. I'm not saying you shouldn't have a business card or a book mark or a flyer with your name on it. But your primary go-to reference should be your website.

   And here's why: as hard as this is to hear, people are going to forget the title of the book, or books, you've published. Or your last name could be something weird like Isbester, so they can't spell it. So they're trying to find your books on Amazon but can't. So they give themselves a mental shrug and walk away, comforting themselves with the thought that at least they'd tried. But if they can put your first name and park benches of South London into Google and if you've done your website correctly, your website should pop up. And who knows, they might buy a book.

   So make your website: www.lastnamepress.com
   or www.shortfirstnameshortlastnamepress.com

   And the headline of the website needs to be the name of your publishing company with the subtitle (but still a headline): A Publisher of Books about the Park Benches of South London

   Then you're easy to find.

   Please note that the headline on the website should contain the word Publisher.

Admittedly I didn't do that, but that's because it simply never occurred to me. And no one told me to do it either. And now that I've chosen Claret Press, I'm not changing it.

Fight the impulse to be clever. The headlines and titles on your website should be simple and clear. Don't translate anything into Latin. Don't make up some evocative neologism, because the only person on the planet who will be able to remember that word is you. Don't hyper-design where there are no words at all and instead books drift in and out of view. And don't use a long and/or rare word that people aren't sure how to spell.

> TRUE STORY: I once did contract work for a company called Cornucopia. It was a lovely place to work and I thoroughly enjoyed my time there. But I spent the first weeks sounding out the name of the company so that I could type it into a message. Corn... I'd breathe.... U.... Co... Pia. And I'm a flipping professional! I shudder to think about what the client had to do to reply. Copy and paste?

I'll share with you something that a consultant friend of mine told me when I started: Never make anyone think. She'd take a look at my website and give a long slow shake of her head while saying, *Katie, I've told you this before, don't make anyone think. It still requires thought to navigate around your website, to read your content, to find your contact details.*

And I'd grumble back: *Not much it doesn't.* But then, I would simplify it further.

So the next obvious question is, how do you get a website?

There are two ways to do this. You pay someone else. Or you do it yourself. If someone else does it then be aware that you will be endlessly going back and forth to that person, asking them to tweak this, add that. So that person had better be very patient and/or very cheap.

The other option is to painfully teach yourself how to do it. I do my own website, using Wix. That's because someone said to me, *It's so easy, you just drag and drop, it's so straightforward, it'll take you a weekend to learn how to do it ... ok maybe a long weekend.*

And I fell for that, hook, line and sinker. It took me closer to five months to figure it out. But once I got it, it became so straightforward, so easy, that I now understand why someone said, *it's so easy*. I can now effortlessly update my website, critically assess how it's performing and tweak its design. And I still only use a fraction of the tools that Wix offers me, although I'm slowly chipping away at that one.

I recommend that you spend the time and the effort to figure it out. This is especially the case if you're a micropublisher. By the time you email somebody, wait a few days for a response, send them an email because there's a typo, wait a few days, etc, you might as well have done it yourself. In the long run, it's just easier (and almost certainly cheaper) to learn to do it yourself.

Plus it's kind of a crossover skill. Once you get it, you can get other ways of using the internet to your advantage. So you might as well buckle down now and teach yourself how to do it.

There are a couple of these platforms where you drag and drop. I have what was considered to be the easiest, Wix, but many people use WordPress and Squarespace. The difference between them seems minor. Pick one. Make it work.

3. **Get Insurance**
   I have insurance for the people who come in and out of my house in the process of publishing. It seems like overkill. But that doesn't mean it isn't wise.

   I get work experience students for a week to a few months. Authors meet me at my house, and we sit in front of the computer and go over things. People, stuck for a birthday present, have been known to bang on my door and snap up a book. I have held book launches (grudgingly) at my house where books are sold.

In summary, people buy things and work for me. This legally changes the status of my front room. Should one of them trip over their shoelaces and crack a limb, I am liable. So I have insurance. It's a legal requirement as well.

There are a number of other things you *could* line up before you start. Here's a short list:

- An IP lawyer (IP stands for intellectual property). Sometimes they call themselves a media lawyer.
- An accountant
- A book designer
- A marketer

I didn't have any of those things when I started and I don't think you need them BEFORE you start.

1E) What's Copyright Anyway?

Before you starting publishing, it's really important to understand copyright because copyright is an asset that your publishing company will own. But we need to unpick the meaning of the word, which is bizarrely complicated and easily confused. Before I do that, I want to strongly emphasise that I am not a lawyer. If you have copyright issues or questions, please go to a lawyer and don't listen to me. They have years of schooling under their belt plus years of experience. For good reason, they get paid for their knowledge, and no one pays me.

Having said that, let me outline something that's really confusing for everyone and that's the word itself: copyright.

In a nutshell, there are two meanings of the word copyright. How confusing is that! Ironically, here we are in the creative industry and we couldn't even come up with two different words for two entirely different phenomena.

Here's Meaning Number 1. Let's call it the Author's Copyright.

Author's Copyright is what the author keeps. That's not up for negotiation by the way. No matter what, the author keeps it. The author can't sell it. Or divide it up. Or lend it to someone. It's not divisible. It's not an asset that can be bought or sold or traded. Not ever. Authors have no option in the matter.

Author's Copyright means that the author will be recognised as the author no matter what. For ever and ever. Regardless of who publishes it, how it is published, when it is published, how it is distributed, the author will always under all circumstances be the author. Sometimes people call the Author's Copyright a "moral" copyright, because this concept of copyright is heavily imbued with an ethic. It's not about money or about contracts. It's about right and wrong.

Sometimes in the front of the book on the publishing information page, you'll see under the copyright sign, the words: *The moral rights of the author has been asserted.*
That is the Author's Copyright.

Not every jurisdiction recognises moral copyright. This matters in other industries like music but not much in publishing.

Now let's look at Copyright Number Two. Let's call it the Publisher's Copyright.

The author grants to the publisher the right to print copies of the work and sell it, and then the publisher and the author share the revenue in some kind of split. What I just described is generally known as a licence. The author licenses the publisher to print, distribute and sell the book. It can be for a limited time period or for a limited territory or for a limited format. It's up to the publisher and the author, that is, it's up to the licence holder or licensee (the publisher) and the person selling the licence (the author). In other words, every licence can be different.

A licence is an asset. It is a tradeable commodity. So the publishing company can sell the licence, for example, to a bigger publisher. In that circumstance, the original publisher no longer prints and distributes and sells the book, but instead sells on that licence to another publisher who prints and distributes the book. I have done that with three books by a single author. I sold the licence to an American publisher larger than Claret Press. I have taken those books down off my website and I can no longer sell them. I'm thrilled. So is my ex-author. These books have been repackaged, given new titles and better distribution in the USA and Canada. I make a small amount of money from this through royalties, although not a lot. But really what I love is that the author gets greater exposure in a different market.

It's also possible to sell off just bits of the licence to someone else. Like the licence to create an audiobook goes to one company and the licence to translate it into German goes to another. I've done that with *Brushstrokes in Time* by Sylvia Vetta. It was translated into German by

Drachenhaus Verlag and turned into an audiobook by Essential Audiobooks in New York. I now can't sell that licence for the German translation or for the audiobook to anyone else. This all seems fair enough to me. Again, I made a pittance and the author got greater exposure. It's a win-win-win.

To sum up: Both are called copyright. But one is a moral right of ownership and has nothing to do with money, and the other is a licence and has wholly to do with money. One can't be sold, the other can be. One is non-divisible, the other can be sliced and diced more ways than a carrot in a Veg-O-Matic.

Now let's make it more complicated. The ability of an author to grant a licence to a publisher expires 70 years after the author's death. This is easiest to understand with an example. Ian Fleming wrote the James Bond books. Once Ian Fleming died, the ability to determine who got the licence to publish the James Bond books was decided by Ian Fleming's estate. This is generally the author's children, or possibly his grandchildren. But once the man has been dead for 70 years, it passes into the public domain. At that point, anyone can republish James Bond books. Anyone can make a James Bond movie or comic book or radio play. The concept and the name and the stories now belong to all of us. In the case of James Bond, that's going to happen in less than a decade.

But remember, moral copyright never expires. So when some publishing company republishes James Bond, it still has to say on the cover that the author is Ian Fleming, or Ian Fleming has to be referenced somehow. For example, in the publishing information at the front of a book it might say, *The character of James Bond has been based on the writings of Ian Fleming*. Or the title might be: *Ian Fleming's James Bond: His New Adventures*. But Ian Fleming's estate doesn't own the copyright and doesn't get a dime from the sale of these out-of-copyright books. Personally I think that that is why they killed off James Bond in the last movie: they had run out of time to make money off the character. So what the heck, kill the man off and now no one can easily utilise him.

Here's a warning if you are thinking of creating a micropress that utilises characters which are out of copyright: some aspects of some characters may have been added on over the years and those aspects are not out of copyright. Winnie the Pooh went out of copyright in 2023 but not his little red top. So if you want to write or depict him, then he has to be as shirtless as Magic Mike. Sometimes aspects of a character can be trademarked like Mickey Mouse's ears. As long as Disney continues to renew its trademark licence, then your little mouse cannot have ears like Mickey's.

Copyright is every author's soft spot. As indeed it is for every illustrator and cover designer. Press on that soft spot and the creator will yelp. It's the nature of the creative beast. Losing "ownership" over their work is their worst nightmare. I have seen small publishers promise authors greater "ownership" (whatever that means) of their work if they sign an extortionary contract. And authors, not knowing what copyright is and incoherent over this topic anyway, sign the contract, profoundly grateful to that publisher.

Not every indie wears a white hat. Sometimes an indie can be a right little shit.

The point of the publisher's copyright (the licence to reproduce, distribute and sell) is that it's something that can be negotiated. As a small indie you might use that knowledge to your advantage. You could offer authors a normal royalty for the first five years. Then the authors have the option to buy the licences of their own titles back from you for a nominal price to self-publish and get the long tail for themselves. How do you calculate that nominal price of resale back to the author? Beats the heck out of me. Or you can give almost no royalty to the author (1% or 2%) but the licence is only for three years, and then copyright automatically reverts back to the author.

There is a problem for micropublishers at the other end of the spectrum. The author goes to some workshop on copyright and comes out with incredibly complex expectations. They'll take a certain % on the first 2,000 copies sold, another % on the next 5,000 copies, and anything over that is a third rate. If it sells in the USA then it gets a fourth rate and of course if it sells in translation then a fifth. And I'm like, *ahhhh... no.*

We micropresses survive by being quite simple, stripped down to bare efficiencies. So I give a % of royalties for anything in English anywhere in the world and another for translation. Neither changes based on the number sold. It's the standard rate, even on the generous side. It means that I can glance at the numbers sold and ballpark how much I've made. It makes my royalty statements easier to compute and explain. There's much to be said for simplicity.

There is another aspect to copyright which everyone should be aware of, and that's quoting from someone else's work. This is quite tricky because this form of copyright is in flux. Driven by sampling in the music industry, the amount of someone else's work that you can use is getting smaller and smaller. An author in one of the books I published had a character singing the chorus from a Beatles song, All Together Now, and we had to turn somersaults to figure out how to do that. We were allowed to quote the title and up to 10 words from the song. Probably by the time this is published, it'll be fewer than 10. So tread carefully.

Now look, copyright is way more complex than I just made it out to be. There's a reason why lawyers specialise in just this area. So if you think there's an issue, for heaven's sake, consult someone who actually knows about it.

This issue of how long you intend to hold the copyright, sell it back or sell it on to another publisher, should be clear right at the start. It should be part of the contract. You should have a business plan of which the copyright is part. When your author asks why, you should be able to explain in simple terms why you need the copyright that you have.

I hope that this explanation has made things a little clearer. I tell you what would really make things a little clearer: if we had two different words for this. But we don't. Instead there is maximum confusion and sometimes hard feelings between authors and publishers. And that strikes me as a terrible shame.

Part 2: ACT

What you need to know about the options to edit, design and distribute a book both in paper and as ebooks.

2A) On Project Management

One of the crazy things about being a micropublisher or a self-publisher is the sheer number of different skills you need. It's outrageous to ask anyone to have them all, much less do them to a high standard. But there you go, that's micropublishing for you.

In a nutshell, publishing is project management. I call it "the pipeline". You start with a docx and you feed it into one end of the pipeline and out the other end comes a beautiful book. It's not particularly creative. It's not writing or painting or acting or dancing. You don't even have to like what you're doing or respect the English language or believe in the power of words.

What it does require is that most things are done in a certain order.

When I started, I created a grid with every step the book took as it went through the pipeline. As the book progressed, I'd tick the box. I could easily see if I missed a step or was doing things out of order. I kept that grid, erasing one title and writing in another, until it became second nature.

It looked a little like this:

Title	Author	Contract Signed	ISBN	Edited & Approv'd by Author	Design'd	Proof-read & Approv'd	Meta-data submit'd	Upload	Test Copy Ordered & Approv'd
Fun With Dick and Jane	Dick and Jane	Yes by both parties	978-1-910461-12-3	Edited: Katie Approv'd by both	Yes	Yes	Yes See attach'd	Yes	Yes
See Spot Run	Spot	Yes with a paw print	978-1-910461-12-4	Edited: Katie Approv'd	Yes	Yes See attach'd	Yes See attach'd	Yes	Yes

There were more columns but the page doesn't have enough space to put them in here. I think I had something like 15 columns. Make your own grid. Add and subtract columns as you need them. I've even had up to five tables but broken down into different stages:

First: pre-publication (contract, author's address, author's bank account for depositing royalty, author's website, author's social media, ISBNs)
Second: design (cover, spine, back, interior pdf, proofreading, illustrations, copyright permission)
Third: creation of the document itself (deep edit, approval, close line edit, approval, proofreading, approval, pdf, epub)
Fourth: uploads to various sites and platforms and/or sending it to the printer (dates, payments, checking it's done)
Fifth: post-production (launch, marketing, press release)

What's key is an obsessive attention to the process. It's not by working hard. Or caring. Or a superior grasp of literature. Horrible as this is to say, that's mostly irrelevant.

This skill is not unique to publishing. I remember reading a Malcolm Gladwell book where he made the point that performance on tests makes absolutely no difference whatsoever to achievement in the profession. The LSAT (the American standardised exam for entrance into law school) only tested whether or not the youngster performed well at law school, not whether the youngster would then have a brilliant career as a lawyer. Gladwell pointed out that, whether performing high or low on the LSAT, the earnings and the professional achievements were the same. Somewhat surprised, I mentioned this to a man I knew who had set up his own law firm. He wasn't surprised. He told me the single best skill to have, the best indicator of achievement bar none, was being organised. As he described what was involved with achieving in law (as opposed to achieving at law school), I recognised them as the same skills as publishing: planning, prioritising, hitting deadlines, integrating critical feedback at the right junctures, signing off steps and pushing through agendas. And that has nothing to do with test scores.

So if you are worried that you can't be a publisher because you lack the knowledge of how to do it, ask yourself this: are you well organised? Can you learn and improve your organisational skills?

2B) Choosing The Format

Let's talk about which format you want to publish in and why; what each format gets you; and when you should use that format.

It's the 21st century. There are choices out there which no one predicted a generation ago. Publishing, more than most industries, has been profoundly transformed by digitalisation. I think that's because publishing didn't really make the small changes throughout the 20th century to keep up with the changing technology. So when Amazon hit in the year 2000, publishing was low-hanging fruit, ripe for the picking. In effect, all the small changes that other industries were making over the decades happened all at once with publishing.

Digitalisation has given us micropublishers and self-publishers. You and me. And it's also given us choices about the formats of the books we can publish: paper, ebook, audio, PDF.

So let's look at various forms of books that can now be produced. On the basis of the kind of book that you choose to publish (its genre and market), the format will become obvious.

1. Let's do the easiest one first: good old-fashioned paper. The vast majority of authors want this. Micropublishers like, even need, to make their authors happy. If you make a beautiful book, then they're thrilled. Also we know that people like to read with paper. The number of people who read ebooks has hit a plateau of about 30% of all books sold. So 70% are still choosing paper. Some genres are best in paper, like art books. Obviously. But also business books. Businessmen like to be seen reading a book, so business books are, by and large, a bigger size so they attract attention. Non-fiction is predominantly paper. Same with textbooks. Kiddie lit is on paper because parents buy it and they want to see their kids reading; kids find it easier to read and retain more if they read on paper; and of course kiddie lit typically has illustrations.

Because of ebooks, paperbacks are now seen as a luxury product. Mass-market genre reads have migrated away from the classic cheap paperback where the pages are so poorly glued in that you leave a trail of them, like breadcrumbs, as you read. Instead, paperbacks are becoming ever more beautifully designed and publishers are now charging more for the pleasure of reading on paper.

This does tend to mean that you need a good, even an excellent, book designer. They're out there. The website Reedsy has book designers. My own book designer is on it and gets work from it and she's done amazing covers. She's also available through me, if you want to reach out to her. Or you might want to train yourself to do it. It depends on the computer programme you have on your computer and your own design skills. I'm a terrible designer and it would take an awful lot of training to get me to the point that my books had the professionalism that I wanted them to have. So I hire someone else to do it.

So ask yourself: Who am I publishing for? What genre am I publishing? Then make sure it fits with paper before you go with paper.

2. The next most obvious is ebooks. Ebook means electronic book. Meaning that it can only be read digitally on a device like an iPad, your phone or a whole range of ereaders: Amazon Kindle, Sony Kobo, Barnes & Noble Nook, Onyx and more platforms turn up every year.

Even people who like paper will read ebooks on holidays, or when they want something to read in the next two minutes. The elderly are increasingly reading ebooks because they can adjust the font and it's lighter to hold. So even if you mostly publish on paper, you might well consider also publishing the ebook. If you've got a professional book designer, then they can, somewhat effortlessly, create an ebook from the paperback. It's not a huge added cost. So why not?

Plus there are some genres that do better as ebooks than as paper, such as crime and romance, which sell more titles than other genres and by a long shot too. So if you are publishing crime and/or romance, then it's entirely reasonable to produce only ebooks. I mean, why would you produce a paperback when no one is going to buy it and it costs money to create?

The standards of ebooks are, dare I say, lower. If there's a typo or a spacing problem, no one is going to complain or even notice. Ebooks are the new pulp fiction. Cheap to produce, cheap to buy.

And that's the sting in the tail. People are hooked on buying ebooks for not a lot of money. If you're just starting out as a first-time author or as micropublisher for first-time authors, it's hard to charge more than a few pounds for them, and likely less. You might even give it away for free. It's mighty hard to make enough money selling ebooks to make it worth your while.

TRUE STORY: I published a page-turning political thriller called *Term Limits* by Steve Powell. It has sold over 2,000 copies, of which 1,600 are ebooks. The ebook sells for $0.99. I have made as much money from the 500 paperbacks as I have from the 1,600 ebooks.

As an author publishes more titles and gets a loyal reading audience, especially if they're writing books in a series, you can raise the price from 99p to £1.99 to even £3.99. Keep in mind that different consumers will buy the ebook at different prices so definitely move the price up and down. Also, once you have a series, you make the first one discounted or free in order to get everyone hooked.

If you focus on only ebooks, then you can really learn how to market them through. It requires more skill with technology and a genuine commitment to marketing using technology, but if you don't mind doing that, then go for it.

Kindle (meaning Amazon) sells about two thirds of all ebooks. It's a higher % in the UK and a lower % in the USA because in the USA there's more competition from other eplatforms, like Barnes & Noble. There are also specialist platforms that deal with just one genre, like fantasy, romance or crime.

So if you are just doing ebooks, I would recommend that you figure out which eplatforms sell your genre, and learn how to upload to each of them. I talked to a self-published author, a rather successful one, who does just ebooks of his crime series and he told me that he uploads to about 20 different eplatforms and it takes him about half an hour. It all seemed very reasonable to him.

You can also sell ebooks from your own website as a Word docx or a PDF or an EPUB. I do this. I have a "shop" on my website from which people can buy the ebook. A few people do. Not very many but enough to make it worth my while.

If you sell your ebook off your own website, then there is an unfortunate reality. I regret to say that the world has some very bad people in it. They can buy your ebook off your website for (let's say) 99p. Then they embed in it a piece of malicious software (malware). Then they give your ebook away on other websites. People download it for free. The malware then goes on other people's computers and steals their data. This happens more often than not with genre reads: dragons, erotica, erotica about dragons. The author is annoyed because their book is being given away. The reader is annoyed because the book has mucked up their computer. It's a lose-lose.

In theory, it is possible to block this by embedding in your ebook something called DRM (digital rights management). This blocks some greedy techie from effortlessly embedding their own evil coding into your ebook and giving it away. It's not entirely successful. It's more like locking your front door. If someone wants to break in, they still can, if they really insist on it. But you've made it more difficult to do so.

The problem with DRM is that it's quite tricky to do. You have to buy the coding off someone else and it's a bit of a palaver. So it's a judgment call about how serious the risk is. Are you creating erotica with dragons? Or is your book about park benches in South London?

3. The third format is an audiobook. I have never heard of an audiobook that wasn't first an ebook, or more reasonably both a paper book and an ebook. There's no reason why you couldn't publish works as solely an audiobook, but it seems not to be done. A few Audible originals are only available as audiobooks, but they are mostly tie-ins or you're getting something more like a podcast.

   Audiobooks are growing at around 30% a year and supply is stretched to keep up with demand. So there's an incentive to do them.

   Again, some genres sell better than others. Crime in particular sells well on audio. Epic stories. Young adult. Biographies. The classics. Romance not so much, but chick lit and women's book club books do better than you'd think. So again, before you decide if this is for you, check out whether or not people are actually buying the genre you publish.

   Audio is also trickier to do than Audible will let on. Quality ranges widely, as does the cost of producing an audiobook. Like most things in life, what you pay for is what you get. So if it is super cheap and seems like an offer too good to be true, then what you're probably sacrificing is quality. If you want proof, just listen to the free out-of-copyright classics you get on LibriVox, all read by volunteers, bless them.

   At the moment of writing (2024) Audible and other big audiobook platforms have blocked computer-generated voices. I recently listened to AI audiobooks and they're not as bad you'd think. There is a noticeable computerised sound to them but it is slight and after about 15 minutes of listening, you don't hear it anymore. And AI-generated audiobooks are really very cheap to produce.

I produce the occasional audiobook with a small audiobook producer. Relative to everyone else, it's both affordable and highly professional — and not AI. I'm happy to recommend them if you want a name.

4. A chapbook is another category that is intriguing. It's not really a paperback or a hardcover, although it's on paper. It is usually a short book, little more than 40 pages and sometimes less than that. They are tiny in size, as thin as a phone but squarer.

   They tend to be beautifully produced, like a piece of artwork. The binding might be hand-sewn and the paper handmade. It might include original artwork drawn on pages so that each one is unique. It's not a book to read as much as to treasure and never ever lend.

   I see them at art fairs or pop-up shops or one-of-a-kind craft sales or high-end Christmas gift shops or on Etsy. They are pricey.

   There is a more cost-effective chapbook. Strategically placed text is photocopied on both sides of a single sheet of paper, and then folded. The folds are then slit to create a pamphlet. Put a couple of those together until you have a booklet. They can be glued together or stapled. They typically are poetry or experimental prose or philosophical teachings. They might be a fable or a kiddie story. They can also be individually decorated.

In summary, before you choose your format, you have to choose your genre, your audience and your own ability with technology and design. Then the format or formats become obvious.

2C) A Traditional Distributor

I have a traditional distributor called Gazelle. I haven't got an unkind word to say about them. They are super nice. I get them at the end of the phone. They reply to my emails on the same day. But we could be in the honeymoon stage because I've only just started with them.

Before that, I was using print-on-demand with IngramSpark and indeed my backlist remains with IngramSpark. I'd wanted to leave IngramSpark for years in order to get better distribution and I was in the process of switching over to a distributor when COVID struck. The negotiations with a small distributor collapsed. That small distributor then went out of business. In fact, COVID took out a few distributors here in England, and England's second largest wholesaler. That gives you an idea of how close their margins were.

Once COVID passed, I once again reached out to distributors. I was looking for the one-stop shop that would give me global distribution for both paper and ebook. I had a good enough track record as far as I was concerned: three to five books a year, year in year out. It's tough with print-on-demand to get found by people who don't already know you so my sales numbers were low, but the reviews were excellent, they were well endorsed by big names, and the occasional one got shortlisted for an award. I rather thought that I was a safe bet.

I thought wrong.

Literally, and I am not exaggerating when I say this, not a single distributor gave me the courtesy of a reply. Not one. I phoned. No one phoned back.

I dropped the scale of my ambition and sent out another round of queries to less-well-known distributors asking if they would be interested in representing Claret Press. Again, not a single response. Down the list of distributors I went, sending out queries, pitching Claret Press.

Finally, I reached the newbies, the smallest of indie distributors, the ones established in one market and now reaching into another. I got two replies and set up two Zoom meetings. At the first meeting, no one showed up. I thought perhaps I'd screwed up and that the meeting was on Microsoft Teams and not Zoom. Nope. The person just hadn't shown up. Perhaps, I thought to myself, we got our lines crossed or a kid had a tumble at school and ended up at A&E. You don't know what's happening at their end. I sent off an email and got back the reply that everything was fine, but they were busy and so had simply pulled a no-show without explanation – but perhaps we could rebook. I elected to return the favour by not bothering to reply.

So I braced myself for the Zoom event with Gazelle. Would anyone even show up for it? Two men did: the manager and the owner. We spent over an hour going through my business, what they could do for me, what I needed to show them. We did the same about two months later. A straightforward contract got signed. Gazelle gives me top-of-the-line distribution for paper in the UK and EU. No ebooks and nothing abroad – I do that through IngramSpark.

Gazelle recommended a printer that was cost effective and with whom they had done business. I checked it out and compared prices and set up a Zoom call with it. Again, we had a prompt and helpful Zoom call, and many more since.

It's the way business is supposed to be done.

Here's how it works:
You print up some copies of books. I have printed up as few as 250 copies of a title and as many as 2,000. They get sent to Gazelle's warehouse. They can sit there for free for two years. If all the copies have not been sold by the time the two years are up then we have to decide what to do with the remaining copies. These are called remainders and can be pulped or sold discounted or donated to charity or used to prop up broken chests of drawers. I don't intend to have remainders. That's why I printed up so few. If I run out of copies, then I can print up more and it takes about two weeks.

Gazelle makes the information about my books widely available to bookshops and Amazon and other institutions. They ensure that the book is in the wholesaler (which in England is Gardners) and there is next day delivery to both Gardners and any bookshop.

There are specialist distributors: business, art, graphic novels, academic etc. who know specifically where to put your books: which bookshops, who to speak to, what part of the world is interested in your books.

A micropublisher needs a marketing plan in place for the distributor to build on. Like everything else, the book business is demand-driven. A distributor builds a demand on a pre-existing demand built by the author and/or publisher.

To ensure that your distributor does its job to the best of its ability, you have to do yours. That means a lot of forward planning. You should know 18 months in advance approximately what you're going to publish. You need endorsements in advance. You need events lined up: launches, bookshops, interviews and shared events. That's hard for us micropublishers to do. We don't have the staff to do all that organising. We don't have the authors with the market recognition for bookshops to agree to a signing.

Undoubtedly that's why no one wants to work with us. We're too last-minute. We haven't the marketing or the forward planning. We've been known to lurch.

Your authors want their books sitting on bookshelves. You can tell them facts like less than 1% of books published in that year end up sitting on a shelf in a bookshop. They don't care. They want the possibility of being in that 1%, which is what the distributor offers. And you've had it with complaints about Amazon listing your books as "Out of Stock" because you're print-on-demand, and friends of the authors being unable to order books at their local bookshop for Christmas. Yes, distribution solves those problems. But it's no panacea.

> Can you afford to put up the money in advance, and if it doesn't sell, can you afford to lose the money?

How many copies should you print up? That is, how many copies of each title normally sell in a 2-year period?

Where are your readers? Are they in Britain and the EU or are they evenly scattered throughout the world? That is, do you have a marketing plan to give to the distributor?

Can you get everything done at least six months before the actual publication date? And by everything, I mean metadata, final draft, endorsements, cover, marketing etc.

If you know the answers to all of the above, and those answers are detailed and you're confident of them, then having a traditional distributor makes a difference. If not, then in my opinion (and I am no expert, let me just emphasise that) I would err on the side of caution and stick with your existing printer and distributor, whether that's face-to-face or Amazon or IngramSpark or some combination thereof.

2D) Only on Amazon

Let us be clear about what Amazon is. It's a "bookshop" that exists nowhere on any piece of land. Also it's a printer of self-published books. And a distributor of everyone's books. It is *not* a publisher. When you say you are publishing on Amazon, you are not. You are publishing. You are the publisher. You are printing and distributing on Amazon.

This is not a detail. This goes to liability in defamation suits and copyright infringements. Let's say you have written a YA fantasy novel. You have put it up on Amazon to be printed and distributed. You are the seller. The book gets pirated. This pirated version also gets sold on Amazon, complete with your cover and your name – only with a different ISBN. Any marketing that you do is undermined by this copycat book. This is not Amazon's problem. Many creator/sellers (not just of books but also of innovative do-hickeys, herbal remedies, dog toys, etc) have tried to get Amazon to stop the sale of copycat goods. Amazon shrugs. That's not its problem.

Equally, let's say that you've published something libellous or violates some legal principle, let's say, pornography. The author is responsible. The publisher is too. The bookshop might be, depending on the situation. Yet if the book is only sold on Amazon, then it is not. While you and the author will have to defend yourselves in a court of law, Amazon will not.

The point I'm trying to make is that Amazon is an entirely new beast. There are few rules it has to follow, and what few there are, get ignored. There are times when this is a good thing. Mostly it's bad, like when it drives bookshops and small- or medium-sized publishers out of business, doesn't pay its taxes and breaks labour laws while getting government subsidies to operate.

Here's a fact that might make you squirm: Amazon is the largest bookshop in the world.

Here's another: Amazon sells two thirds of all ebooks.

And a third: Any place there is internet, there are ebooks.

So if you are interested in getting loads of readers, then Amazon is part of the answer. I'm not saying that its actions are right and proper. I'm saying that this is a reality.

Amazon's self-publishing arm is a print-on-demand service. That means that you upload your file to Amazon, it holds your file in its cloud and, when someone goes on to the Amazon website and buys your book, Amazon then prints it and mails it to that person (unless it's an ebook when Amazon simply sends it to the person's Kindle). The turnaround time for the printed book is about two weeks. If the book is really popular and loads of people are buying it, then Amazon might (but probably won't) stock it. There is so little profit made from a book and books take up so much space that Amazon, which started out explicitly as a bookshop, is now trying not to stock books. Oh, the irony.

Amazon has tried to close the circle by occasionally publishing self-published authors on only its platform and then promoting them.

> TRUE STORY: I know of an author through a friend. He wrote a few thrillers for a mid-sized publisher. Sales declined over the titles published. Although he was a competent enough writer, he was dropped by his publisher. So he self-published a few titles. Then Amazon offered him a contract for his next thriller. Delighted, he signed it. Amazon published him and his next book and even his third, put his books on banners across its website. He sold like hotcakes. Then he got dropped again due to declining sales. He's not unhappy about that as apparently, he sold something like 100,000 copies and can now sell more profitably as a self-published author.

At the risk of stating the obvious, Amazon plucked him out of the slush pile because some algorithm said to. And the algorithm was right. It was a win-win for both him and Amazon.

The Amazon ebook used to be formatted differently from the rest of the industry. Amazon's ebook format is called MOBI. As in Dick. Strictly coincidental? I think not.

The rest of the publishing world uses a format called EPUB. Any designer can create an ebook in either format. That's not a problem because you can now upload your ebook to Amazon as an EPUB.

There are a host of videos on how best to upload to Amazon and how best to make Amazon work for you. Amazon has more than one kind of publishing available to micropublishers, and there is a skill to utilising it. A complex skill.

Do not believe Amazon when it says it's easy or simple or straightforward to make money from using just Amazon as your printer-distributor.

I'm not saying that Amazon lies because that's not true either. It's more like caveat emptor.

Amazon has the best marketing I've ever seen. It's so good that you won't even know it's marketing. Friends of mine helpfully send me articles published in reputable newspapers about the glories of Amazon. They were little more than free advertisements repackaged by some journalist who needed to file copy by Friday at 5pm. But you really have to be knowledgeable about publishing to see that.

So let's cover what's good about Amazon:

- It's relatively easy to design a book, get it printed up and distributed through Amazon only. Look, I am neither a designer nor a techie nor under the age of 25. And yet I figured it out. If I can, then really and truly, so can you.
- Amazon has a complex ecosystem. There are promotional campaigns. There are discounts and bonuses. There are ways of packaging it to appeal. You can easily change the price up and down. But you do have to learn how to use Amazon fully. And you know what it's like: there's the apprentice experience and

then the journeyman and finally you become the master. Once you've got it, then you can reap efficiencies and utilise the system to your best outcome. I would recommend that you buy a book on the topic and/or watch a zillion YouTube videos and then try it with zen-like patience and good humour.

- You don't need to constantly compare and contrast printers to get the cheapest deals, learn what kind of cover template the printer wants and tweak your design to match. This is just time consuming and kind of annoying.
- You don't need to waste time chasing distributors. Again, time is precious.
- You don't need to put up much capital in advance, relative to other ways of getting books out. This is a low-risk option for publishing. It means that you can make mistakes without being overly punished for it.
- There is almost no need for storage space because it's print-on-demand; just print them up as they're needed.
- You get a global reach.
- If you find an egregious typo or you need to update the book, then you can do that simply and without informing anyone. It'll cost you to update a new file but that strikes me as fair enough.
- You get a monthly statement with money in your account that month. It is, near as I can determine, the only company that does that. The others deposit money after the financial quarter.
- There are a ton of supportive videos on YouTube and Reddit to guide and help.
- You get a higher rate of return if you only use Amazon, a significantly higher rate. A high-enough rate that it could make the difference between being in the red or being in the black.

And now let's do the downside. Because there's always a catch, isn't there?

- There are plenty of people who simply refuse to use Amazon on point of principle even if they have an Amazon account. I'm one of them. There are people who get all their paper books through their local library or bookshops, neither of which will bring in an

Amazon-only book (turkeys don't vote for Christmas). This is equally true of ebooks. Many libraries and bookshops now have ebooks, and they use a different format than Amazon's ebook format. Can you afford to lose those readers? I can't. Further to that, my authors like to know that the local libraries and bookshops can stock their books. They get flinty-eyed if that's not an option.

- Having the book only available on Amazon screams self-publishing and there's a taint to that. Does that smell bother you? It bothers me because I am not a vanity press. I pay authors royalties, they don't pay me. I have a filter. As a traditional publisher I do not want to be lumped in with the self-published.
- Amazon's self-published books all kind of look the same. Those who read a lot might know this, even if it's at a subconscious level. See above about the taint of self-publishing.
- When there's a problem, there is never anyone to contact but instead endless chatbots and computerised answers. And you think to yourself: *If I could just explain this to a person and have that person tell me what to do, then I would learn how to solve this problem and it would likely never happen again.* Dream on.

I'm not entirely convinced that Amazon advertising works. If you read this book cover to cover, you will discover that I say that about pretty much everything. As in: I'm not entirely convinced that Facebook/Twitter/Amazon/Google/Instagram/Fill-in-as-appropriate advertising truly works. A few years back, I spent a winter taking courses, reading books and learning how to do Amazon advertising. I'm a clever lass. I was reasonably confident that I could do this. I spent £200 advertising a single book. I sold one ebook for £3.99. Not exactly the ROI that one might have hoped for.

Be aware that some genres might do just fine using Amazon-only printing and distributing, like crime and romance. Other genres, not so much, like art history. Be aware that some books produced by Amazon can look just fine, like crime and romance. The look of other books, not so much, like art history. I make this point because what works for one micropress, might not work for you. Know your genre. Know what your genre's books look like. Know where your genre's readers get their books from.*

How do you know what your genre's books look like? Go into the largest bookshop you can find and hang out in the section that holds the kind of books you want to publish. Take photos of covers. Take your tape measure or a ruler and jot down their dimensions. Flip through them and see how much white space they have and end notes and front matter. Study the people who are buying them. What's their demographic? How many are they buying? Try not to get arrested.

2E) IngramSpark

IngramSpark is owned by Lightning Source, which was a print-on-demand printer and distributor for big publishers. It still is. In fact, as I write this, it is setting up a new wholesaler to compete with Gardners in Britain and it is trying to set up a print-on-demand for just micropresses or small indies. Lightning Source is a colossus. It's not as big as Amazon but then again, nothing is. Nonetheless, it's absolutely massive. IngramSpark is the print-on-demand arm for self-publishers and micropublishers. That is, for you and me.

I have used IngramSpark and continue to use it on a selective basis. I have the most experience using it compared to using a traditional distributor (which I also use) and Amazon (which I used to use).

I want to put my cards on the table and say that if you are just starting out, IngramSpark is the best place to begin.

Having said that, it might not be right for you and your books. And IngramSpark is a long way from perfect.

So let's start with the obvious. Like Amazon, you upload files to IngramSpark. The files are held in the cloud. When someone wants a book, the title is printed and mailed out. The turn-around time is about 10 days to two weeks. They say it's less. It's not.

Here's the big difference: distribution.

IngramSpark has paper distribution into bookshops, including specialist bookshops, across most of the world, as well as into Amazon. This means that people can go into their local bookshop, whether it's a big chain or a small indie, and order your book. It won't be found sitting on a shelf waiting for a browser to stumble across it. But equally you won't have to give much money to the bookshop for the service of bringing in your book (35% of RRP; 40% of the RRP if the person orders it in the USA). It's not taking up shelf space. It's a guaranteed sale. Ordering a book through a bookshop brings people into it who might not otherwise have gone in, and that means that the bookshops might make an additional sale. So they are not hostile to it.

IngramSpark sends your paperbacks and hardcover books through to Amazon too, so people can tell you that they ordered the book through the bookshop and would never, under any circumstances, order anything from Amazon ever. You nod and thank them. You get the monthly statements. You know where the books are bought.

IngramSpark sends ebooks to specialist platforms as well as into Amazon. The % that you get back from selling ebooks is small, although it's consistent with other platforms. The % that I get back from ebooks is 40% of the RRP. If the book's price is £0.99 then I get back £0.37 (I lose a little in the transmission costs).

IngramSpark can also distribute the book into libraries, although again someone has to go in and ask for it, and the library has to agree to buy it for its patrons. This almost never happens to me. Sigh.

Like Amazon, there's a ton of information about how best to use IngramSpark so that it really performs for you. I recommend that you set aside an hour a day for a week and systematically trawl through all the instruction videos up on YouTube. Make sure that you use the more recent videos as all these platforms change from time to time so how best to use them can also change.

So let's look at the advantages and disadvantages, which overlap with Amazon's self-publishing arm. Here are the advantages:

- You don't need to put up much capital in advance, relative to other ways of getting books out. This is a low-risk option for publishing. It means that you can make mistakes without being overly punished for it.
- There is almost no need for storage space.
- You get a global reach.
- If you find an egregious typo or you need to update the book, you can do that simply and without informing anyone. It'll cost you to update a new file but that strikes me as fair enough.

- It's the one-stop shop for paperbacks and ebooks. Time, my friends. This is all about saving time. And a one-stop shop is a great time-saver.
- You don't need to constantly compare and contrast printers to get the cheapest deals, learn what kind of cover template the printer wants and tweak your designs.
- You don't need to chase distributors.
- Theoretically, your books can be in libraries and bookshops. This means more people might stumble across them, which means that you sell more. It also means that the taint of self-publishing or being with the world's most humble publisher and not Penguin Random House almost entirely disappears. Not quite, but you have to have a very finely tuned nose to sniff it out. Authors appreciate that. I appreciate that.
- You get a monthly statement of what has sold where and via which platform and in which format.
- It does all your metadata across all the platforms so that you don't have to do that multiple times.
- If you want to change the price then it happens once every few days which really is often enough in my opinion – although it might take as long as two weeks for the price change to go through the system.
- The system is (compared to everything else) quite simple to use. I put a premium on simple to use. I've had it to the back teeth with learning new ways of using systems better.
- If you're ordering a stack of books to be sold at an event either for yourself or for an author, then it takes less than 10 days for them to arrive. I think that's pretty good turnaround. This is in England. It might be different in different countries, like the USA and Canada.
- You get the long tail of sales. So long as a title sells for years and years, you're earning money. I intend to sell books until I die. And who knows, maybe I'll break even on titles eventually.
- There was only once when the printing was off and IngramSpark immediately reimbursed me for the cost of those books (once I had sent in photos and videos). Let's put this into context: since I started helping people get their own work published, through my sister company, Clapham Publishing Services, and through

Claret Press, I must have printed up literally thousands upon thousands of books. And for only one printing to be messed up with the pages cut wrong and the printing going off the side of the page, that's not bad.

Now let's look at the other side of the coin:

- IngramSpark over-promises and under-delivers. Don't believe its propaganda.
- Libraries resist buying IngramSpark books because it is a self-publish service. I'm not saying that they won't. I'm just saying, it's very unlikely.
- Canadian bookshops won't bring in IngramSpark books. I don't know why. I just know that it's impossible to get my books into Canada through IngramSpark.
- Books don't always print up correctly when ordered in other countries. For example, I published *Learning German (badly)* by an English author, Tim Luscombe, who was living in Germany. It's not actually about learning German. It's about identity and Brexit and where he belongs. It's funny and heartfelt and insightful. His German friends wanted to buy it. Yet every single copy ordered in Germany came up squiggy, the ink from the letters running into each other, like it had been printed by a drunken racoon. IngramSpark clucked sympathetically but told me that they had nothing to do with the German printer and it was up to the Germans to get it right; IngramSpark makes no promises that the printing will be successful, only that it makes the files available in Germany. I believe that's called "terms and conditions". I cried from sheer rage. Finally, someone at IngramSpark spoke to someone in Germany and a button got pressed and it all went swimmingly well. This took months. Multiple phone calls. Emails. Searches on the internet about printing. **Months and months**. I rather think that if IngramSpark says that the book can be printed in Germany, then the book had better be printed in Germany by a sober racoon.
- What's the one time of year that everyone wants books? Christmas. When is there a long turnaround time for printing up a book and getting it into a bookshop? Christmas. So your books

won't be bought as presents. Is this a problem? Only if you want to sell books.

The largest brick-and-mortar bookshop in Britain is the chain Waterstones. The man who runs it, James Daunt, also runs the chain Daunt Books and the chain Barnes & Noble in the USA. So this following piece of information might be true on both sides of the Atlantic. Waterstones brings on extra staff at Christmas. They are not trained. When a customer goes into a Waterstones and asks for an IngramSpark book the staff can't figure out how to order it. I spent a depressing Christmas phoning around Waterstones in various locations in England: Leeds (a city), Bury St Edmonds (a small town), Clapham Junction (a busy intersection in London) and so on. I phoned nine different locations. I got told that they couldn't get the book, it was out of print and to get it through Amazon. One – and only one – person said that it could be brought into the shop for me to buy within a reasonable time period. When I took this to IngramSpark they asked for the names of the sales clerks I had talked to at all these Waterstones. Because it's the clerk's fault. So well trained staff, or staff who have been there for a long time, or staff who don't have anything else to do and have the time to figure things out, they can bring in IngramSpark books. But at Christmas? No. When do people want to buy your books? Christmas.

- When you upload your file to IngramSpark and the information is sent through to Amazon, it says "Out of Stock" on Amazon's page. This is entirely reasonable. The system is demand-based. If there hasn't been any demand (and there hasn't been because the book hasn't yet been published) then Amazon is going to reflect that. If the book has low or even moderate demand, then the book will not be stocked at Amazon, and the Amazon page will still say "Out of Stock". This is confusing for people who want to buy it and think they can't because it's not in stock. It infuriates authors who think that you, a micropublisher, really ought to give Jeff Bezos a good talking to. There are ways around this, none of which particularly works. You can explain this to everyone. You can say at launch parties and events and through social media and on your website and on the author's website to ignore the "Out of Stock" status and order it anyway so that it will be in stock. Or, at the actual launch party, have someone go around with an iPad and have people log into their Amazon account and buy the book through Amazon rather than taking home a copy that evening.

- The cost. Per unit, it's pretty high. So you can't really order five copies for yourself. You might as well go to a bookshop and order them. It'll cost about the same but the bookshop will make some money and the whole creaky demand-driven system will work better for your title.
- IngramSpark will send you a monthly statement about the amount of money that you earned that month but it won't give you the money until three months after the end of that month. So let's say you sold a bunch of books in the first week of December in time for Christmas. But you won't see that money until April. This is industry standard. But it's not how things should be done. IngramSpark is a big company. It can afford to pay micropublishers at the end of the month.

Again, like everything else, you have to ask yourself if IngramSpark is appropriate for the kind of books you are publishing. Do you need international distribution if you sell only in the UK? Do you need to have your books readily available at Christmas or do you intend to sell throughout the year? Do you plan on using bookshops to sell or do you intend to sell face-to-face or off a website? In other words, who is buying from you and when and why and how?

I keep coming back to that question because once you've answered it, many other things fall into place. So if you aren't certain if you should print up stock and sell it yourself, use only Amazon or IngramSpark, then go back to the beginning and ask yourself basic questions:

Who are my buyers?
Why are they buying their books from me?
How do they find my books?
How do they pay for my books?

2F) Do It Yourself

This is a quietly more successful technique than most micropublishers realise and I suggest that you pause and reflect on this option.

The first thing you need to do is find the people you want to sell to. Your tribe. Your community. And then you sell them what they want. To put it another way, the marketing comes first.

It's easiest to understand through examples. So I'm going to give you three that I have had personal experience with. I'm sure you can come up with others.

A friend runs a pop-up shop and you help her. Over time, you get a feel for the people who buy from your friend. She has a newsletter so that people who buy from her know when the next pop-up will be and where. You print up half-a-dozen titles that these people would be interested in: romance, how to decorate on a budget, fashion icons, etc. You have small print runs of 150 copies. And if the book sells really fast at these pop-ups and through the newsletter, then you print up another 150 copies. In the process, you collect their email addresses and when a new title comes out, you email them a newsletter about it with pretty pictures.

You (or a friend or just about anyone else) have a small podcast about technology and science, the marvels and wonders of the world that is about to happen. You have guests on. You field questions from a phone-in. You get a clear idea of what people are grappling with. You start a sci-fi and popular science publishing company. You use the podcast to inform everyone about the books, and bring on the authors as guests. You sell from the podcast's website. Now change the topic to sports. Or make-up. Or baking.

You're a consultant. You're a cabinet maker. You're a teacher. You're a trainspotter who spends hours blissed out at trainspotting conventions. You're a political activist obsessively following the X/Twitter feed of dozens of commentators and journos. You're a gardener whose garden is open to the public once a year in June. You love everything Japanese and take language courses and have a black belt in judo. You have an uncanny knowledge of the Napoleonic wars or Kurdish carpets or Dresden figurines.

Find your passion. Build your tribe of like-minded people from your passion. Know your tribe's likes, drives, questions, frustrations, confusions and hobbies. Find the books that speak to that.

Commission books, print them up and then sell them to your tribe. You don't need a distributor. You don't need Amazon. You don't need IngramSpark. You need a newsletter and enough space to store boxes. You need a website and a way for people to buy from your website, that is, a shopping cart.

You need a vision.

> TRUE STORY: There's a publisher in the outskirts of London who publishes solely on the boats of World War II. He does about five books a year. He goes to specialist shows, re-enactment events and fairs about WWII. There he sells his books, collects emails from those who are interested and gives talks about boats of World War II. He sells them to his newsletter subscribers. He sells out. He makes a profit.

With this model, you choose the scope of your own ambition. It can be quite modest. Equally, it can grow and grow.

Here's an example of a micropublisher that became quite impressively large without ever using Amazon, IngramSpark or a printer and distributor. It's called the Folio Society and it reprints both fiction and non-fiction but gloriously illustrated. Imagine *Lord of the Rings*, but with a tooled-leather cover and gilt-edged paper and a ribbon for marking your spot. And the story itself would be richly illustrated with full-colour original artwork. The books cost (ka-ching!) so the number sold is not high. But since all sales are through the company's website, profit is high. The Folio Society advertise with inserts inside upscale magazines, like the Times Literary Supplement.

Here's the only thing that I would recommend you do. Cost it out. It's a bore but contact each and every printer that you can find and ask them to give you a costing for:

- 75,000 word book
- Standard size of Crown B
- Cream paperback
- Black and white interior
- Colour cover
- 70gsm weight paper
- Delivery to one address
- 150 copies
- Reprint cost for another 100

Now look, use your noggin. If you are printing up recipe books with a spiral binding, then compare the prices for that and not for a paperback. If you are printing up children's illustrated books then ask the price for a colour interior. If you are doing big hardcovers, then ask for the pricing for that.

I'll pass on a bit of gossip. Without exception, every small publisher I know who has worked with any company based in China ends up leaving their Chinese printer. There are a range of reasons from hidden costs to wrong colours to supply chain problems. So beware the super cheap Chinese option.

Finding your tribe and publishing for them is not so useful if you're an omnivore and know a lot about lots of different things but nothing in any great depth and simply can't find a tribe. Or if you cycle through the passions, obsessed about one thing for five years before losing interest and moving onto something else. Or if you don't have any capital to risk, because even the best publisher for their own tribe will occasionally get it wrong and publish a book that doesn't get read. Then that poor person is stuck with 150 copies and has to sneak around the back of restaurants at 2am, sliding copies into their rubbish bins, rather than paying for pulping.

So there are limitations on when this works and why it works, and reasons when and why it won't.

As for me, I keep a small number of books on my shelf and sell them to people who like to buy off my website. But Claret Press publishes too widely to truly be able to narrow down a tribe. So it doesn't work for me particularly well.

But I can easily see how it could.

Part 3: ACCOUNT

At the core of every business is money. If people are paying you and/or if you are paying people, then you are running a business. Money management is essential to ensure that you can continue to publish.

3A) Accounting and Royalties, that is, Money

Look, money's an awful topic. I don't want to write about it for the same reason that I don't want to discuss my age, my youthful indiscretions or the sheer number of vapid vicars who ensure I stay snuggled in bed on a Sunday morning. We all know these things happen. But we don't talk about them.

As my kids say, hold my beer.

But first, I want to emphasise that you don't have to publish for money. Micropublishing could be a wonderful adventure for you. Some people golf and others travel. Some people have a small fortune in shoes sitting in their bedroom closet. You publish. If it loses money, you can live with that.

Whether you need to be profitable or not is irrelevant. You need competency in money management. Taking care of money cannot be handed off to a good friend (as I tried to do) or to an intern (as I also tried to do) or done after everything else is completed (again, that's me). Money starts and ends and is in the middle of every micropress, every project, every activity and every title. Get it right and no one notices. Get it wrong however...

Whether your micropress is a charity or you're running a writing co-op or you've created your press as a small business, it's critically important that you put money at the very centre of what you are doing. I'll pass on a piece of advice from an 87-year-old lady who lives down the street from me. Although born working-class (her father drove a milk lorry between Cornwall and London) and not educated past high school, she became a successful entrepreneur, a multimillionaire. I asked her for any tips about how to achieve in business. She said, *Check your bank account daily.*

I puzzled over that. I get monthly statements. Why would I check my bank account more often than that? And then I realised, if you do that, you are lingering over the money side of the business, fussing about it — and on a daily basis. That's a good thing.

When it comes to listening to someone about money, I'm not sure I'm the ideal candidate. I can't hand-on-heart say that I break even, because I don't pay myself. I make money by selling my editing skills to authors who self-publish or want to find an agent or a big American publisher. I have expanded that sister company to include other publishing services for people who self-publish such as coaching, book design and copywriting. That props up Claret Press. Buying this book helps to prop up Claret Press. (Buy a copy for a friend! Give it as a Christmas present to your family! Own multiple copies for yourself!). My goal is to get Claret Press to stand on its own two feet and be a viable business entity in its own right.

However, as someone who is not particularly interested in or skilled with money management, I'm going to share with you the lessons I've learned.

So let's start at the beginning with bank accounts. I have a business bank account with Santander. Initially I used a range of banks that offered their services for free. But charges would later kick in (FREE!! for the first two years) or there were hidden charges for normal services (no cheques, no cash deposits, no mailed statements) or they had a reputation for getting hacked on an astonishingly regular basis. I found that switching between banks was a massive headache, and clients from my editing service always seemed to pay into the wrong account.

So I settled on one bank. Santander has the best reputation for small businesses, and it has worked fine. The only fly in the ointment is that it charges me to put my money in its bank. It's not a lot, about £100 a year. But I've found that a steady trickle of money leaves me monthly. You'd be surprised how much money can exit an account even when it's only a trickle. I never haemorrhage money. But I can never fully staunch the outflow either.

It's up to you which banking system you use. But I think it's good business practice to have a separate bank account solely for your publishing. It offers clarity. It acts as a boundary (you won't accidentally dip into it at Christmas). It professionalises you psychologically.

I'm the sort to lick the end of a pencil and scratch out the royalties on a piece of paper, then laboriously type them into an author's royalty statement. It would take three weeks, working long into the night, to figure out the royalties for a handful of authors.

That's just dumb. And if that's how you do your accounting then I'm sorry for just insulting you. But it's still dumb.

The only way you're going to survive as a micropress is if your computer does the work. Your computer imports the figures, crunches them and spits them all out. The only time you lick a pencil tip is when you have a craving for graphite.

There are free accounting programmes as part of Microsoft Office. Google has something called Google Sheets. I have used them. They're like a dumbed-down version of Excel. If you can figure out Google Sheets, then you can figure out Excel. If you are using Google Sheets and they're working just fine for you, then stick to them.

There are a range of accounting packages for small businesses. And if you can't figure out how to use them, you can easily hire someone off Fiverr to do bits and pieces of it for you. My experience with these packages has not been wholly successful. They're close but no cigar. I find that the time it takes to learn them is extensive, and they're not quite as useful as I think they're going to be. Plus I don't know what to tell the Fiverr guy to do because I'm lost myself.

> TRUE STORY: Neighbours of mine run an impressive ironworks design studio in London. Her husband does the engineering, she does everything else. This includes the accounting. She has gone through all the software packages, including Sage. She's a clever clogs, adept at running a successful small business. Her experience with accounting packages is that

if it's one rung higher in the ladder in terms of complexity, or one rung lower and not complex enough, then it doesn't really work, not really. She'd just commissioned a bespoke piece of software that fulfilled her specific accounting needs.

It's Goldilocks. Your accounting package has to be just right.

So I thought about this and then talked with my kid who was studying engineering at university. I asked him to write me a piece of software that was "just right". The final goal was that I would press a button and my royalties would be done. I'd press another to know how many copies of each title I've sold (print or ebook or both) or whether a title has broken even yet or where the books are being sold (UK or USA or EU) or how my expenditures break down.

He's a nice kid, sufficiently forgiving that he's still talking to me. But the process of him learning how micropublishing works so that he could write the code made it a slow journey. I sweetened it this year (our third year of doing this) by giving him £1,000 for services rendered. I suspect a more accurate amount would have been 10 times that.

Nonetheless, I thrill to press that button. Sometimes I just play with the numbers because they look pretty; my son has colour-coded everything and made pie charts and a line graph that goes up and down depending on which button I press. It's fun. That's worth £1,000 to me.

There's an important principle as to why you want your accounting to be state-of-the-art. Number crunching is not for the tax man. It's not for the authors. It's not about whether your micropress makes a profit or a loss. That information is the by-product.

Number crunching is a tool to create useful information. For clarity, bookkeeping is keeping the record of money in and out. Accountancy is understanding what all that data means.

You keep track of whatever you want. You then use that information to make informed decisions about how to go forward, and where to put your time and capital. To that end you need to keep track of:

1. All the costs
2. All the income that is earned

Here are some of the things I've learned:

- I break even on the long tail, not in the first two years of sales. I need more like five.
- Non-fiction sells better than I thought it would.
- I need to raise the prices of my books. When I sell books in the EU, the prices are higher so I can break even. Here in the UK, we are selling our books at too low a price. The low prices benefit the Big 5 because they can price us indies out of the market. The Big 5 set the "normal" price and then we feel morally obliged to match it. But we're not the Big 5. We're small and we do not have the economies of scale. And besides, our competition is not the Big 5 but Netflix and gaming. So raise the prices on your books.
- My costs are going up. I've started investing more to make Claret Press more effective and efficient.
- If you want to grow your micropress and move from print-on-demand to some other format and distributor, then you need to show your numbers. The better your numbers, the more likely it is that you'll get a distributor and attract the support of the wholesaler.

Having said that, I don't keep track of all the costs. I only measure costs for which I get an invoice: my fabulous book designer, uploading files, mailing out copies of a title, printing up copies of a title, the website host, the domain name, computer ink and paper, a new whiteboard every couple of years, the entry fee to London Book Fair, coffee if I take an author out, beer if I take an intern out, a train ticket if I have to travel to see an author and so on. It's a surprisingly long list of things you spend money on in the process of publishing books.

I should also be measuring all sorts of other costs, such as:

- Renting a room in my house
- Heat and electricity and broadband
- The time to edit the books I publish
- Talking on the phone with people involved with publishing, whether that's an author or another business
- Reading submissions
- My time at the London Book Fair and other book fairs

Mostly these costs are time related. I work for free.

I decided not to measure the cost of me for the simple reason that I don't know how to. It's especially confusing when I meet a friend of a friend for a coffee to discuss books in general and her book in particular, publishing in general and publishing her in particular. We might chat about the sad state of the world and agree on how to set it right, her kids, my kids and the kids of our mutual friend. Is that social or business? Is it work or pleasure? I've decided it's pure pleasure – because it is. As is my time at London Book Fair. As is editing. I've been editing now for 25 years and have won awards for doing so. It's a genuine pleasure for me to edit (mostly). So I struggle to know how to measure the cost of that.

The bottom line is that my bookkeeping is not an accurate assessment of the cost of running Claret Press.

If you don't have access to a kid who can code then I recommend you find one. Seriously. Hire off Fiverr or Elance or Upwork or any number of other platforms. Ask your local accountant to recommend someone who can do it for you. Skip the frustrations of using a not-quite-right software. Go bespoke. It'll pay off if only by making your life happier and easier and more efficient. Not to mention the fun you'll have playing with coloured pie charts.

3B) What is Metadata and Do We Need It?

The short answer: yes.

The longer answer: maybe.

So what is this thing called metadata? It's all the information about your book. That's it.

It's the title, author, publisher, ISBN, number of pages, date of publication, format. Metadata says whether or not there are illustrations and how many and whether they are in colour. It's the size of the book: the length, width and depth and occasionally the weight. It can include a table of contents, a preface and who wrote it. It includes reviews and endorsements. It includes other books that the author may have written and the author's bio and links to the author's website. It can include an extract. And here's the really important stuff: it includes a short description, which is generally around 250 words, and a long description, which can be really very long indeed. It includes the genre and the sub-genre, known as BISAC and Thema codes. It includes the setting, if that's a special feature. It includes keywords.

You need to have all that information about your book out there on the internet so that people can find your book through various search engines and eplatforms. In order for that information to be put on those search engines and eplatforms, you need to buy access. It's not free. It's called "buying metadata". But you're not buying the metadata. You're the one supplying all that information. What you're buying is the ability to have that information up on the internet or sent to bookshops.

Let me give you an example from my own publishing. I published a memoir of a lady whose life rather impressively mirrored many of the changes in post-war Britain. Sylvia Vetta was born to a working-class family from Cornwall where her meals were dominated by traditional fish and chips (homemade), scones and cream (again, homemade) and seasonable fruit and veg. She married a man of colour, absorbed the tastes of his homeland and made friends with people from other countries who introduced her to their cooking. As a device to tell her story (and through her, the story of post-war Britain) each chapter had an authentic recipe. The book's title is *Food of Love*. As in: *If music be the food of love, play on*.

The book was put in the cookery section of bookshops because my metadata wasn't good enough. I had to tweak my BISAC codes, change my keywords (the title is a keyword so I had to override the word food) and alter the descriptions. Yes, publishing can be that irritating.

Before you decide that you don't want to do publishing because you just can't be asked to spend your time doing such things, let's see if you even need to buy metadata. Here are three situations when you *don't*.

First, you sell to your own subscribers. They already know the kind of books you are offering, that's why they subscribe to you in the first place. So you don't need to buy metadata.

Second, you sell face-to-face through local fairs and street auctions, church events and social clubs, Christmas parties and book launches. This is how I mostly sell, which is why I was able to resist buying metadata for so long. My authors and I are almost permanently active, pitching up at every event possible to flog as much as possible. People would show up to hear someone give a lecture on beekeeping or buy some crafts or mingle with their friends, and end up buying one of my books. It kind of works.

Finally, you sell only through Amazon. When you upload your book through its self-publishing arm, Amazon offers it to you for free.

Let's say you're like me. You started off selling face-to-face and now you're selling more widely. These new people who find your book through word of mouth or through the internet seem like icing on the cake. Besides, selling more widely is only reasonable. You've already made your book available, so you might as well do as much as possible to make it findable. That's a jargon word, by the way. Findable. Also known as discoverable.

For people to **find** or **discover** your book on the internet by happenstance, and perhaps then buy it and perhaps then follow your author or your website and perhaps then buy more books, you need metadata.

This is what you do first and you can do it for free.

1. You give as much metadata for free as you possibly can to your book distributor because why not. If they want to know your books' weights, then weigh your books and input the data. If they want to know how many different places are referenced in your books, reference them all. And so on.

2. Do the same for Bowker in the USA. That's Bowker.com; it's free. Bowker will send it to all the bookshops and libraries in the USA.

3. There is something called Nielsen Title Editor in Britain. It will hold all your metadata. It will send the basic information to the bookshops in the country.

These are the big three. It's important to get it right and get it updated regularly. And I mean regularly, like once a month or so, or more often if you have new information.

Don't do it more often than once a week though, because it takes that long for the systems to send information out and for it to churn through the various databases. So before you start inputting new data, double-check that the old data has gone through and become the new normal. I do this by checking the listing on Amazon and Waterstones and Barnes & Noble. If it looks the way you wanted it to look last week, then you can update the information with new stuff. If last week's updates haven't yet been processed, then you have to drum your fingers on the desk impatiently until it does. Then and only then can you update it again.

So you have to pace yourself. Write it into your calendar so that once a month you update everything. It might be an endorsement or a new book out or a cover for a book that you're going to publish in four months. Things like that get put into metadata. If you have nothing to update, then you go onto your next task for the day.

Now here's where it gets complicated. And it's really only complicated if you're British. We have to buy metadata to get more than just the title and author into Waterstones, the biggest bookshop in the UK. And keep in mind that you are not trying to get your books to physically sit on the shelves in Waterstones because that's unlikely to happen. You just want to get your books fully listed on its website with the endorsements and the descriptions and the keywords.

The free service that Nielsen offers only covers the title and the author and the ISBN.

Nielsen offers packages where you pay to get one, 10 or 50 titles with full metadata per annum. All that metadata then goes off to Waterstones. Many people who don't want to buy off Amazon, buy instead off Waterstones. The question is, how many people browse on this platform? My experience has been that people browse on Amazon and then buy from Waterstones or Bookshop.org or their local bookshop. If they do that, then they'll already have the author, title and maybe even the ISBN. So you don't really need to have complete metadata on Waterstones or Bookshop.org so long as Amazon has your metadata.

So buying Nielsen's enhanced metadata to get more information on Waterstones' website is a judgement call. I use Nielsen's enhanced metadata for my newest books. I only publish a few books a year. So really, I only need to buy metadata for 10 titles worth a year. That's the package I buy. And then I switch around the titles that get the enhanced metadata.

Here's how you get your metadata into libraries and other bookshops for free:

You set up accounts with a British company called Stison. While this is completely irrelevant, I have met Mr Stison himself at the London Book Fair and he's a lovely man. The company Stison (not the man) turns the metadata into something called an ONIX file. This is the file that goes to all the other bookshops except Waterstones. You can even upload it to Bowker in the USA. You then give that ONIX file to BDSLIVE who send it out to bookshops and libraries.

It's a bit of a bore to do, to be honest. And tricky. But once you get the hang of it, it takes about half an hour once every few months.

And then there is more metadata out there for your books to be found or discovered or stumbled across, and then bought. It's a half hour well spent.

3C) What are Comps and How to Use Them

Here's the theory: You have a book with considerable appeal if only people knew about it. So you give away copies to reviewers at appropriate newspapers or influencers or other gatekeepers, such as teachers or professionals in the field. These people will review it, and this will create a ripple effect such that it becomes a must-read.

These free copies are called comps, as in complimentary copies, as in freely given away with no strings attached.

I like the theory. It makes sense. Or at least it used to. I've heard a story. Let's say it's about *The Girl with the Dragon Tattoo* by Stieg Larson (2005), but it could have been about any similar book. The publisher was a smaller indie in an era before Nordic Noir was even a term. According to the story, 250 hardcover copies got printed up and handed out. At least some read it and positively reviewed it. And the rest, as they say, is history.

That was then, this is now.

I have a friend who worked for the BBC. It has a room so stuffed with unasked-for books that staff could just take what they wanted. So she did, from gorgeous hardbacks to the latest releases from bestselling authors. Once, I hired a table at my kid's school's Christmas fair thinking that parents will buy books as Christmas presents. What I didn't know was that a schoolchild's father worked at a newspaper. He scooped up all the comps: picture books, glossy art books, latest releases by bestselling authors, hardcover history books. He had two long trestle tables buckling under the weight of all those books, they spilled on the floor underneath and were stacked behind. He was selling them for a pound each. People left with bags of books. And his table still buckled with what was left over. This man then gave all the money to the school, which was decent of him.

Do I need to tell you that no one bought from me with my full-priced paperbacks.

What happened between 2005, when a publisher could distribute the advance copies of *The Girl with the Dragon Tattoo*, and now?

What hasn't changed would be a simpler answer. Self-publishing, Amazon and the exponential growth of the number of books published per annum. Netflix and streaming. Better video gaming. Audiobooks and audioplays. Substack and subscription eplatforms. And that's just what you pay for. Plus all the free media like YouTube and social media platforms.

The grip that books had as the best and most convenient form of entertainment and intelligent engagement is broken. Publishing now has an awful lot of competition.

Bloggers and reviewers in newspapers and magazines, indeed everything out there, all compete furiously for eyes. The ability of even established and respected reviewers to get you sales is dramatically reduced. Don't get me wrong, reviews are still important for endorsements, for prestige and for the sales they do generate. But reviews should be seen as part of a larger marketing campaign, rather than the sole end.

It's incredibly difficult to get your books reviewed in a national newspaper without a connection. I haven't got any and as a result the only book I've had reviewed in a major newspaper was because the author had been a journalist and favours got called in.

Obvious exception to the rule: Let's say you have published a celebrity, even one that only occupies the C List. Or even a D-Lister. If they're on any list, no matter how far down, then you might get a newspaper to review it. They're looking for eye-catching copy, and your minor celeb might help them sell a paper. Life's unfair that way.

Social media is a different kettle of fish altogether. Influencers and reviewers on social media tend to like to have hard copies to wave around and take photos of. And fair enough too. Social media is a visual platform as much as anything else. So you have to put a limit on how many you send out. It's up to you how many copies you donate. Many Claret Press authors send out up to 50 copies of their own book to bloggers and vloggers, bookstagrammers and influencers. Ouch. If the author is thinking strategically about building a career as a writer, then this might be considered to be an investment in the future. What if you decide to take a leaf from the publisher of *A Girl With A Dragon Tattoo*? Then that's 250 copies you give away. Super ouch. But you might decide that's a good investment.

Distributors, which make their money as a % of the RRP every time a book sells, don't like to give comps away. That's not why they set up a warehouse and developed a distribution network. So Gazelle, my distributor, will send off 10 to 12 copies and I pay for the postage. I send out comps to get endorsements, which usually is a PDF but sometimes is paper. Look, if you give me a good reason why I should, I'll send you a comp.

There is a digital comp service that you might want to explore. It's called NetGalley. I am sure it has competition and copycats, but NetGalley is the biggest and best known. The author or publisher pays NetGalley an amount, which varies depending on the service, and the PDF is available for free for anyone who wants to read it. In exchange the reader offers a free review, which is posted on Amazon, their own website and maybe also a bookshop's website. Typically, the PDF is made available to readers a month or so before the actual publication date. Then, on the day of publication, all the reviews are uploaded to Amazon so that the book starts off by being well reviewed.

Like many marketing schemes, this works best with genre reads where everyone knows what they're getting and there are a lot of readers of that genre: romance, crime, fantasy, sci-fi, self-help, chick lit. It's not as useful for history, business and non-fiction in general, and downright counterproductive for literary fiction and specialist tastes.

NetGalley is especially useful when the author is a first-time author and has no following. Here's why: You've put a ton of metadata out there about the book. You've invested in a fabulous cover. There's an endorsement from a well-known person on the cover. Someone is browsing on Amazon or the internet and types in the key words. Up pops the book. It all looks pretty good. The potential reader checks it out and sees only one review and it's clearly from the author's mother. So the potential reader remains potential. If, however, there are 25 reviews of it (26 if you count the mother's) and these reviews are thoughtful and critically engage with the book, then the potential reader might turn into a real buyer. They might then write another review.

Using NetGalley assumes that the author wants a career as a genre writer and is willing to invest in developing that career. So it's not for the one-hit wonders.

The micropublisher has to work with the author to decide how many comps they send out and who absorbs the costs of them. It tends to reflect the author's own ambitions, the genre of the book, the kind of publisher you are, the depth of your pockets and who you can touch up for a sparkling review. This needs to be judged on a case-by-case basis.

3D) What's an ISBN and Do I Really Need One?

Here's the executive summary:

If you only publish on Amazon, then you don't need an ISBN. If you only sell to your family and friends, or through your subscription list, then you don't need one.

But if your book is to be bought through a bookshop, then you do.

Now let's unpack all that.

Let's say you belong to a writer's group and once a year, you publish a couple of books. Maybe it's a collection of poetry or short stories cherry-picked from the group's writings. Maybe it's someone's novel or memoir. You intend to display these books at the local street fairs as much as anything to attract more people to your writer's group and if you're lucky, sell a copy to a complete stranger. The cost of producing these books is covered by having the authors buying them for themselves and their families and friends. You don't need an ISBN under this circumstance.

Let's say you run a café and you produce a cookbook of your most beloved recipes. You intend to sell it from the café to your own customers. Your customers have also handed over their contact details so that they can be informed of any special deals you might be offering or to book a table or to keep up on your news. You send out an email to them and those who pay online are mailed a copy. You hope that this will cover the costs of producing the book and also cement loyalty to your café. You don't need an ISBN for that.

Let's say you have written a travel memoir of backpacking through a foreign country. To your utter astonishment, no one is interested in publishing it. Screw the publishing industry, you think, and self-publish it. It's only up on Amazon. You don't need an ISBN for that.

In other words, you can publish without an ISBN so long as you operate OUTSIDE the publishing system, that is, you give the book away or you sell face-to-face or through Amazon.

Otherwise, you need an International Standard Book Number or ISBN.

A typical ISBN for Claret Press is 978-1-910461-XX-X
978 – means it's a book that you read as opposed to an audiobook that you listen to
1 – means that it is in English (usually)
910461 – is the code assigned by Nielsen Book Data to represent Claret Press
XX – this 2-digit number means that I bought 100 ISBNs (you can also buy them in blocks of 3 and 10 and 1000 and 10,000)
X – this is just another number

Who knew.

The ISBN is how the publishing world speaks to each other about a specific title in a specific language in a specific size of book in a specific format. Bookshops don't track books through titles or authors. They use ISBNs.

ISBNs are sold through a single entity in every country. In the USA, it's Bowker. In the UK, it's Nielsen. In Canada, it's ISBN Canada. In Australia, it's Australian ISBN.

Plug into Google: buy an ISBN UK (but only if you live in the UK. If you don't live in England, Scotland, Wales or Northern Ireland, then don't write UK, instead write in your own country).

Be canny. There are intermediaries who will help you get an ISBN for a small fee. You don't need them. Go to the ISBN distributor for your own country and buy directly from it. It's cheaper.

The more ISBNs you buy at one fell swoop, the cheaper per unit it is.

The ISBN encodes all sorts of information about it: title and author and publishing company. If you buy the ISBNs, then you are the publisher. So if you and your bestie both self-publish your own books and you decide to share expenses, and if one has written a sexy vampire romance and the other has written a how-to-use-empty-beer-bottles-to-build-sustainable-housing, the publisher will nonetheless be the same. If you're the one who buys the ISBNs, then it's you. If your bestie does it, then it's that person.

If you plan on building a publishing company with a clear brand and sell books to a specific demographic, then you really shouldn't share ISBNs. But if you do it anyway, what's the fallout? Absolutely nothing. Technically, it's not advised. But being a publisher is not advised and clearly that's not stopping you.

The ISBN will also encode the format. So if you are publishing the same book in different formats, then you need different ISBNs. So let's say that you plan on doing a paperback and an ebook. Then you'll need two ISBNs per title. Let's say you decide you also want it as a hardcover. Then you need three. You then decide that it'll be great in a large print format then you need a fourth. And so on.

You can correct typos and keep the same ISBN. But you have to change the ISBN and assign a new one to a title if you:

- change the size of the book
- make substantial changes (perhaps you've added a preface)
- you've kept the text the same but changed the title or author
- bought the title from another publisher

I would recommend that as a micropublisher, you have ISBNs. It means your books go into the catalogue of Books in Print. It means you are professional. Your books can be entered for awards. They can be stocked, bought and sold through a bookshop.

Finally, I would warn you to be careful about registering your ISBNs. Once a number is registered with Nielsen Title Data (or Bowker or any of the other entities) then that's it, it cannot be changed, no matter how unreasonable the situation. Let's say at the last minute you change the title: you need a new ISBN. Or the author pulls out despite having signed a contract or you decide to walk away from the entire book, then you cannot reuse that ISBN. Or you decide not to do the ebook version after all; you cannot reuse the ISBN.

I have wasted a good few ISBNs in my day.

3F) What To Pay For

Our scarcest resource is time. Here is another hard reality: good help is hard to come by. Put those two realities together and it's a recipe for overwork.

There is an obvious solution: you pay someone to get really good at one aspect of what you do so that you don't have to do it. I believe they call it the division of labour. I'm all in favour of it. I also believe that having highly competent staff is essential to grow.

There's only one small glitch: money. The margins are so thin in publishing that you cannot afford to pay a decent wage for anyone competent.

I pay one person regularly: my book designer. She is patient, brilliant, kind and highly affordable. We've formed a mutual appreciation society which continues to this day.

I don't really pay anyone else. I get paying work for my proofreader through my sister company, Clapham Publishing Services, and in exchange she proofreads some of Claret Press's works for free. My kid does the accounting. The British Library is my free business mentor. My friends act as a sounding board for whether or not I should publish something. If I am exceptionally lucky, a clever youngster will pitch up seeking work experience and the chance to acquire some wisdom, which I am happy to provide. Most go on to careers in publishing, using Claret Press as a springboard to a paying position. Sometimes they say, *I have now realised that I never want to do publishing* and I think triumphantly, *Hurrah! I've saved another youngster from a life of poverty.*

There is no doubt in my mind that businesses need money to grow. Claret Press is on a meagre diet and rather than being slim and pretty, it's scrawny and half starved. Steve Jobs once intoned: *Stay hungry.* I dunno. A decent meal regularly consumed is not to be sneered at.

I once had lunch with a very impressive environmentalist who heads up an international umbrella organisation of green NGOs. We were sharing notes. Like me, her organisation ekes out an existence, doesn't pay her but does overwork her. Like me, she gets the occasional clever youngster and is astounded at the difference that makes. Like me, her greatest crunch is time and the stress that induces. We agreed that if we had more money, we'd do the invisible investment, build the infrastructure to stand stronger and be more capable, achieve more and more easily. It's impossible for her to get funding to do that. I don't see it happening to me either.

So I drag my too-thin company upwards, snatching an occasional calorie boost. Steve Jobs also said: *Stay foolish*.

In that regard, I'm doing Steve Jobs proud.

Part 4: ASSESS

Being a micropublisher is about more than measuring things with versions of a ruler. Assessing is the act of judging, of weighing up your needs and of acknowledging the cost of not meeting them. It's a transcendent grope for something intangible that translates into the tangible.

4A) Book Submissions

This chapter might not be for everyone. If you are in a writing group or running a writing course, if you are publishing as part of an outreach for your company, if you are publishing just your own work, then you can skip this. You already know who you're publishing and there is little to no weighing up of options or filtering needed.

If, however, you're like me, then you will eventually get to the point where you accept submissions from complete strangers. Maybe this is in addition to your own writings and your friends' output, but you are also actively seeking to add to your list of authors.

So how do you go about doing this to make sure that you get an author you like and will earn you money? Or at least break even.

I'm going to say two things that are contradictory about how to choose a book to publish. The first is to publish people you know. The second is to publish people you don't know. And neither one is as obvious as it seems.

Let's start with publishing people you know. Many microbusinesses are dependent on the goodwill of their friends, family and broader community in order to survive and even to thrive. So if someone you know, or a friend of a friend, has an unpublished manuscript and it's halfway decent and halfway towards the kind of book you want to publish, then you take it. You will reap the benefits, albeit in a way that's hard to quantify, but they'll be there. People will recommend you on. They'll show up to your book launches. They might simply invite you to dinner and pour you a drink. Or all of the above. In other words, it pays to recognise your community.

And it's not just strategic. You're not an abacus weighing up the value of your social network. You're doing this because you're genuinely happy to be contributing to your community. You do this because you like these people, and you want to be of service to them. Your little publishing company may not Penguin Random House, but it is making your corner of the world a little bit nicer. Pat yourself on the back for that. Raise a glass to yourself and give yourself a quiet nod of approval. You deserve it.

You're also doing this because it's just plain fun. It's fun to meet with your friends and friends of friends to get their books out. If this wasn't fun for you, you wouldn't be doing it at any level.

It's really important to recognise the fun factor because when it stops being fun, you stop doing it. If you're not enjoying an author or their book, then that's a warning bell going ring-a-ling. You may not know why but something is telling you that it's not a winner and you don't really want to do it. The reason doesn't have to be more coherent than that. Trust your gut and stop what you're doing. Re-evaluate and re-think things.

If you decide it's the author you can't work with rather than the book, then you need to find a polite dodge, a white lie. We've all made up pleasantries ('Love the haircut!' 'Of course quitting your job was the right thing to do.' 'He's a real sweetie, you'll be so happy together.') For the sake of common decency and kindness to others, you need to find a persuasive pleasantry that allows you to escape working with people you don't want to work with. Then you can continue to bump into them at the post office and supermarket and parties without any problem.

I have discovered that people who write tend to be really very nice. I have rarely encountered people I can't work with. Sure, once or twice. But that's it. The vast majority of people are a pleasure to deal with, and it's a pleasure to publish their books.

What if you don't like the book but the author is a dear friend? Then you have a judgement call to make: Do you publish it anyway? That consideration is tempered by other considerations such as, is your friend willing to get it professionally edited so that it is improved? And edited again. And again. In other words, a professional editor pulls up the quality of the manuscript until it hits a good enough standard. That process will cost your friend money but that might not be a problem. How many copies is your friend willing and able to sell? If you can break even, then why not publish it; friends are more precious than pearls. Does your friend have more books that will need to be published by you? If the answer is, "Yes indeed, a sizable number are sitting in the bottom drawer," then you need to hit pause. But if this book is a one-off and it's unlikely that your friend will write another, then perhaps you can publish it despite its flaws.

If you really can't bring yourself to publish your bestie's book and she won't pay and she won't market and she won't stop flipping writing, then you've got a problem. A narrow brand is useful. I have said on more than one occasion that the topic doesn't meet the brand.

I have also been honest. A bestie who writes beautiful short stories, wrote and rewrote and rewrote again a novel. It always needed another major draft. She wanted me to publish it and I was forced to say: you don't actually want to be a writer, despite your evident ability. You're seeking closure on this story, which (spoiler alert) mimics your own life. Since you couldn't get it in reality, you're writing it instead.

There were enough grains of truth in what I said that she forgave me. Usually lying works better and I recommend it.

What happens once you run out of publishing the manuscripts of your social circle? Then who do you publish? From the slush pile, you choose unknown people, total strangers. But how do you choose between them? You have no way of judging between them because they're all first-time authors. What criteria assist you to choose?

When you are looking for a new author, you want someone you can work with, someone who gets the fact that no one earns money from this. You want an author who will treat your time and skill and commitment with the respect that they would extend to any other professional. You want someone who will take on board what you are saying to them and make the changes that you deem necessary.

You don't want someone who changes their mind halfway through a 3-book contract, or someone who operates under some kind of an illusion about who and what you are and insists that you have an entire marketing team and a secretary and a rights agent at the snap of your finger, which you are inexplicably not deploying for their book.

The best way to gauge that, in my opinion, is as simple as the submission process. There is a reason why it exists and has been the staple of the publishing world for a very long time. (Qualifier: I must admit that I have been known to break these rules, so these are really just rules of thumb.)

So here are the four things that strongly suggest you have an author you can work with.

1. The manuscript is polished and ready for publication. If it's not, don't go near it. There is nothing to say that the author will ever finish it. There are a surprising number of authors who get close but no cigar. It's like they almost don't want to finish it.

   Instead they phone you up and talk at length, maybe even take you out regularly for a lovely alcohol-laced lunch. You become their muse, their confidante, their port in the creative storm. And that's a big mistake. They don't need a publisher. While it's rather nice to be needed, you fall into the trap of being their therapist or sharing their fantasy of what the book will be once it's done. It's hard to extract yourself because you believe in the book and you understand the creative journey is a tough one and you're a nice person so you want to help. Besides the author has a superior wine cellar. But you cannot be all things to all people. In 99% of the cases that I know of where this dynamic has happened – and boy, is it surprisingly common – the book has not happened. To be a micropublisher, you need to focus on the publishing part of the equation, and not on being the stimulus to completion.

2. The second thing you want to avoid is authors who don't have a clean manuscript. That is, the manuscript is incorrectly formatted with poor grammar and spelling.

I don't mean a typo here or there, I mean basic grammar mistakes. This means that it's not been edited at any level, which means you'll have to do it and that means multiple rewrites, which is a giant time suck and there's nothing saying that the author will accept your changes. You could end up in negotiations with the author like it's the MidEast Peace Talks. I've edited books for decades, had my books get shortlisted for or win awards and had them be published by the Big 5, and I'll still have to do gymnastics to persuade someone — who has never published anything — to make a change.

Equally, a rough draft with poor grammar and spelling might mean that they don't really read that much and therefore don't know what's correct English and what isn't. People who don't read tend not to write cleanly. It's a complex skill, writing, and the best way to learn how to do it is to read, read, read.

So a rough manuscript is like a canary in a mine shaft, one which has croaked.

3. You want to avoid someone who hasn't looked at your website and doesn't know what kind of books you publish or who spells your name wrong or who sends you five chapters when you asked for one, etc. That means that person can't be bothered to do even the bare minimum of effort. And you just don't want to work with someone like that.

4. The final thing you should look for before you even look at the manuscript is the cover letter. Is it professional? Does it do its job? If the cover letter doesn't capture your interest, then why would the book?

This is what you're looking for in the cover letter:

- It's one page. If they can't get it onto one page, then you don't want to publish them. It means they lack control over their own writing.

- Genre. An astonishing number of authors don't know what genre they've written. Which is a problem right there. Or they get too clever by half and insist that the work is so unique it doesn't fit a genre. Or they list every single possible genre that the book could be: it's a horror rom-com coming-of-age adventure with aliens. Which is just unhelpful.

  If you belong to the younger generation, think of the genre as a hashtag. Get the hashtag right and it says more than its few words.

- The cover letter should contain, as its first statement, that the author is submitting the final edited/polished/critiqued manuscript of XX number of words of YY genre. And then its grab is to pique your interest. So the first paragraph is:

  > Please consider for publication my comedy thriller entitled *A Very Important Teapot*. It has been professionally edited, is complete at 75,000 words, and is the first in a series. It's as if Terry Pratchett wrote James Bond.

- Having captured your interest with the grab or tagline, the second paragraph is the synopsis of the plot. And it has to engage. This is your elevator pitch. This should make you think, *ooooh I might want to read that.*

  > Dawson, forlornly courting Rachel (who is smitten with a boring solicitor called Pat Bootle), is delighted when he's offered work in Australia. The arrival of a teapot with a code hidden in the lid makes him suspicious. Other parties join the hunt for the teapot's code: a local mobster, Pat Bootle (who is actually from German Intelligence), a Russian hitman and a British official being blackmailed by the Russians. Meanwhile, Lucy Smith, an MI6 employee, flies to Australia. Dawson and Lucy, kidnapped by the Aussie mob, are rescued by Bootle, and then by the Aussie cops. The story concludes at a disused mine in Victoria where the meaning of the teapot's code becomes explosively clear.

  Ah yes, you think, *this is your classic comedy set up. Everyone is someone else. The hapless hero. The chase involving everyone and his dog. It seems to end with an explosion. A love interest with Lucy. Looks like fun.*

- The third paragraph is why it fits with the other books that you publish, so that it augments and reinforces your publishing brand. The author might name-drop bestsellers similar to their own book to reinforce that this book is not a risk to the publisher and that there is an appetite for this kind of read.

   > As this book uses humour to critique the trope of toxic masculinity it fits well with your books that highlight women's issues such as *Daisy Chain* by Justine Gilbert. With its plot twists, chase scenes and murders, my book would be a good match for the Julie Anderson's mystery thrillers, *Plague, Oracle* and *Opera*. It would appeal to the same readers of bestselling author, Stephen Clarke and his spy spoof, *The Spy Who Inspired Me.*

- Ideally, the final paragraph is something about the author that helps sell the book. Not something irrelevant like how many cats the person has but genuine reasons why the author is the only person who could have written it and what they bring to the table above and beyond the actual text. For example, and I base this on someone I know who now writes kiddie adventure stories, in his younger days the author was a filmmaker of outdoorsy stuff from walking across Africa to climbing mountains to training with soldiers. So the man knows what he's talking about with adventuring.

   Equally if the author has any special skills with marketing, that always goes down well.

If you like the first paragraph of the cover letter, you read the rest of the cover letter. If you like the cover letter, you read the extract. If you like the extract, you request the full manuscript. If you like the full manuscript, you contact the author. If you like the author, you discuss what each brings to the table. If that goes well, then you discuss publication. These are dominoes, one after the other, toppling over. In other words, the brain decides, strategically and thoughtfully and in full knowledge.

That's the theory. Here's what really happened when Steve Sheppard submitted *A Very Important Teapot*: I was organising a charity fundraiser hosted by the amazing Tracy Chevalier, bestselling author of *A Girl with a Pearl Earring,* among so many others. (Unrelated aside: she's the nicest, most down-to-earth person you'll ever want to meet.)

I'd hired an experienced event organiser to do the work. Six weeks before the event, she started ghosting me. Five weeks before the event I came to the jarring realisation that no one had done anything, and the event organiser did not have the courtesy to tell me that a better paying gig had come along. Also, the fundraising event was during the first week of December, the busiest time in the publishing calendar. *Disaster!* was the word that came to mind, although it wasn't the only word.

It's safe to say that I was somewhat stressed and anxious and exhausted. Organising this charity fundraiser was all I did in those weeks – except for one lunch hour when I checked my emails. There, sitting in my inbox, was an unsolicited manuscript. This is what he sent me in its entirety.

> Dawson's forlornly pursuing the lovely Rachel Whyte. But Rachel is engaged to local solicitor, Pat Bootle.
> Then Dawson's best friend sends him to Australia to "await further instructions".
> Why are secret agents from three countries and half the Aussie underworld chasing him?
> Why has Pat Bootle turned up in Australia?
> Who is the beautiful but mysterious Lucy Smith?
> What's the teapot's secret?
> And how do guns actually work?

Cute, I thought. Sufficiently cute that I wanted to write him a nice rejection letter and so I clicked open the submission so I could quote a few lines from it. The first 25 pages made me laugh aloud. I had about 50 minutes left on my lunch break and spontaneously decided to read a little more. So I emailed him to ask for the rest. Please note that at this time I had no intention of publishing it. I just wanted a tiny temporary release from the terrifying disaster looming before me.

By coincidence, Steve Sheppard was checking his emails. He immediately sent me the rest of the book. I read my way through my lunch hour, and even took a few extra minutes to finish it. I still had no intention of publishing it because I don't publish comedy. On the other hand, I felt lighter than I had in a long time.

So I did what I always do when I like a submission. I phoned Steve up and had a chat. I highly recommend this as the next step after finishing reading the submission.

Do you like them on the phone or over Zoom? Are they personable, friendly, open? If you can, invite the author for a day out to meet with you. Do you like them in person? What do your interns/partner/bestie think of the author?

Steve and I had a great chat on the phone. I laughed some more. He's very funny even in conversation. I told him I'm the wrong publisher. I told him to get an agent or a different publisher. He told me he'd already tried, and no one wanted him. I told him how to write a proper cover letter. He told me he'd already done that, and it hadn't worked either. I told him again I was the wrong publisher.

Then I invited him to London for lunch. I really shouldn't have but I like laughing.

In the conversation that you have with the potential author, be honest and open about what you are offering to do for the book and what you expect out of them. For instance, I told Steve that I could edit it and put a great cover on it and distribute it, but I really couldn't sell it and that would be up to him. I also told him that my goal was not to lose money on his book and that should be his goal too.

You don't have to be best buddies with the guy. You just have to be confident that the author is someone you can work with.

If, at the end of the chat, warning bells are ringing and the red warning light is blinking on and off, then you need to back off and send them a nice rejection letter a few weeks later.

That's not what I did with Steve. I sent him a contract. I've now just published his third thriller and I'm still the wrong publisher for him. I am however almost breaking even with his titles. So that's something to smile about.

So this chapter has offered you two ways to choose between book submissions: the right way using cover letters as a filter, and the way that is perhaps less wise but equally beautiful where you publish what you want. I have done both and both have ended well, or well enough. As a micropublisher you can do things that the big guys can't, you can publish whomever you like. You can follow your heart.

4B) Contracts: Coffee or Fences

I'm going to start by reciting an old saying. It's an American saying, so afterwards I'll have to explain it in exhaustive detail, thereby sucking any joy anyone might get from it.

The saying is a joke and it goes like this: A contract and a quarter buys a cup of coffee.

Meaning that a contract is useless. Because the quarter buys the cup of coffee. Of course, a quarter doesn't get you that anymore. You can barely get a coffee for five bucks now. For the sake of argument, let's say that a quarter does.

Are contracts really so useless?

When all else fails, contracts are a final safety net. Contracts are useful if you need to take someone to court. The court enforces contracts. In other words, contracts have a disciplinary element to them. If someone violates a contract, then a disciplinary force (i.e. the judiciary) ensures that what was contracted, happens.

This only works if you are prepared to use that disciplinary aspect, that is, to sue someone for breach of contract and take them to court. Almost no one in publishing is prepared to do that. In effect, a publishing contract is unenforceable. This is why a contract and a quarter buy you a cup of coffee. That's all it's going to get you in life.

I'm going to suggest that you use contracts with your authors despite that.

The first thing we have to do is change the way we think about contracts. Rather than thinking of them as an instrument to sue someone, think of them as a guide. They spell out the rules of the game; they detail how it's all going to work.

A contract can just state the following:

1. Who is doing what. Insert proper names as they are on passports and correct addresses.

2. The title of the work with a two-sentence description of it. This is because the name of the work can change.

3. The number of words approximately. You can be as broad as between 50,000 and 60,000 words.

4. The date that it will be handed to the publisher and what happens if the author doesn't get it to the publisher by that date. Nothing might happen. In this case don't threaten the author with dire consequences. Make the date provisional.

5. The date that the publisher will get it out to the public, that is, publish it. And what will happen if the publisher doesn't get it out. Generally, what happens is that the copyright reverts to the author.

6. Who is responsible for the book design. Generally, this is the publisher but with micropresses you might work together on it. If so, list who will do what and by which date. This includes who is responsible for any illustrations or artwork that the book might have. Decide who gets the final word in the event of a disagreement. With my books, I have the final say.

7. An agreement that the author has not previously published this work elsewhere in part or in whole and will not in the future sell this work in part or in whole. Is this not obvious? Do I have to explain this one?

8. The countries where the publisher has the right to sell the author's book. Is it just the UK? Or every English language country? Or every language everywhere?

9. Does the publisher have the subsidiary rights. Subsidiary rights are when the book is sold into another language or adapted into a movie or audiobook or theatre play or abridged for a different publisher and so on. Sometimes the author keeps the subsidiary rights, sometimes the publisher gets them and sometimes they move between them. This must be sorted out before you start publishing.

    Let me give you an entirely plausible example: You, as the micropublisher, might only have the paperback rights. Another micropress which specialises in ebooks has the ebook rights. And the author, who is really a frustrated actor, is going to do the audiobook himself. So the author has to know that they then can't print out the book at the photocopy shop on the High Street and give it away to everyone who buys the audiobook as a bonus gift. I know that this sounds overly obvious but make it clear anyway. Write it down.

10. If the work defames anyone then the author is responsible. That is, it's not the publisher's fault that the mass-murdering evil bad guy is the spitting image of the author's ex. And if the ex is so outraged that he threatens to sue, well, that's the author's problem, not yours.

11. If, God forbid, the publisher goes bankrupt or dies or the author dies, what happens next? Generally, when the author dies, the author's estate gets the royalties. I once had an author ask if she could leave me the royalties in her will, which I politely, but with considerable gratitude, declined. If the publisher dies or goes bankrupt, it's more complicated. If the publisher dies then the business is sold or folded up, and it's up to the estate what to do with the rights. If the publisher knows that they are going bankrupt, then generally they quietly fold up shop and work out deals with their authors on an ad hoc basis.

12. Who pays who where when why and how. That is, when are royalties produced, what % does the author get and how the author will be paid. And make it clear in the contract how that % is

calculated. It is before taxes? Is it a % of the net receipts or a % of the RRP? This must all be crystal clear.

Equally, if the author wants a special-but-expensive photo for the cover which you're unprepared to pay for, then the author pays for that and is responsible for all the fees and paperwork. Or if the author doesn't have a bank account because he's living off the grid and wants to be paid in cash, then the author has to pay for the sheer irritation of that. And so on.

13. You both should promise to abide by the rule of law. It sounds like a silly thing to have to promise but I have in my life met plenty of people who, I'll learn over the years, have no intention of playing the game by the rules. They think that people who do so are chumps and get mightily peeved when they're forced to. You'll want to avoid those people. But if you don't know this in advance and sign a contract with them, then you want to be able to jab your finger at this clause and say, *You promised you'd abide by the contract and the rule of law in this country.* It helps.

14. Make another obvious statement that the author keeps for himself the moral right to be identified as the author. Why is this necessary? I hear you ask. It's because editors frequently do more than just edit. They can rewrite scenes, add a character, change the ending. The book then becomes a bestseller and gets turned into a movie. Then the editor pops up saying, *Actually it was me, I'm the one who wrote it.* And the author goes, *No way!* Again, this part of the contract resolves a problem before it even arises. The author is the one who wrote the book. The editor edited it. The publisher published it.

Put everything and then some in the contract. Let me give you another example. The author gets a couple or 10 or 20 free copies. You know, the freebies. Spell out even those things. Don't leave it open to discussion. Let's say your little publishing company has subscribers. They get the latest releases for 10% off but if it's a signed copy then you sell the book to your subscribers for the full price. During discussions over the contract, you tell the author this and the author says, *Sure I'll sign 100 copies, no problem.* When the books arrive however, the author is in the middle of a move, is going on holiday, doesn't have the space for 100 copies, runs out of time and so on. So the 100 copies never get autographed. If the author has signed a contract, you can tap your finger on the relevant clause.

The contract is a polite way of reminding people of what they had earlier promised to do.

Once the contract is signed, everyone knows where they stand and what they have to do and what the date they have to do it by. Before it is signed, walk your authors through it. Discuss what works for them and what works for you. That's the whole point of the contract: to create reasonable expectations and boundaries. Tell them you can be flexible on certain things and that you want them to be happy, and that this contract is a mechanism to help make that happen. That the contract can be fine-tuned to the specifics of the situation. And you mean it.

In this way, a contract can be a good thing. So instead of saying that a contract and a quarter buys you a cup of coffee, I'd reframe it as something else altogether. I'd say instead that good fences make good neighbours. I prefer that approach. I like to get on with my authors. A good contract helps you to avoid disagreements and confusions so your relationships stay intact, and you can all focus on producing books. Which really is the point of it all. We all need friends and colleagues, not ex-friends or former colleagues.

You can write this contract yourself. But then run it past a high street lawyer just to make sure that it's all, you know, legal. Or you can buy a contract off the internet (www.buyacontract.com). Even then I recommend that you run it past a high street lawyer. For everybody's sake, you want to be confident of what you're sliding across the table to your authors.

I print out two copies, one for the author and one for me. I sign and mail them both to the author, asking that one copy be signed and mailed back to me. I like to keep the paper copy along with the electronic copy; a contract is too important to solely entrust to a computer.

4C) How to Edit your Authors

I've been editing for 25 plus years now. I started off with doctoral dissertations and academic texts because I used to be in academia and quit, but my friends stayed on. They needed another set of eyes, a trained brain and, since I'd already been well published by university presses, we all had the confidence that I actually knew what I was doing.

That's how I discovered that an astonishing number of academics secretly write detective stories. When you think about it, it's not surprising. Professors like a puzzle, think logically and can put things together in different ways which shed light on situations. So I ended up editing a lot of murder mysteries.

My career grew from there. I'm unapologetically immodest about my authors winning awards, being shortlisted or getting contracts with big publishers.

So when you edit for your micropress, you have to ask yourself hard questions:

- Do you have the competency to edit this book to the standard you want it to be?
- Does your author understand that the edit may not be a comfortable experience?
- Do you manage expectations so that you can get the MS to the standard you want but with minimal unpleasantness?

Here are some suggestions about how to do that. And look, what I'm about to tell you is more rules of thumb and has nothing to do with grammar, diction, style sheets, formatting, character arcs, plotting points and thematic coherence. If it had been about that, then I would have called this segment, How to Edit. But it's called How to Edit your Authors. Emphasis on the word AUTHORS. They're people and you have to work with them.

I was once at the London Book Fair listening to a panel of authors who had all worked with micropresses or small indies or had self-published with paid editing before hitting the big leagues. What completely staggered them was the hard-core editing that the Big 5 did. The authors were poleaxed that the editing experience was an editor telling them at length and in detail what they were doing wrong and what they had to do to make it right. It was less of a discussion and more of a dictat.

You can't do that. You can have high standards; I certainly do. But you have to work with the authors to persuade them to produce the quality that you would ideally like to see, while keeping them completely committed to your little publishing house. A bit of diplomacy does wonders. Sometimes shovelfuls of diplomacy. Actually, just back up the lorry.

Let's first be honest about the reality of being a micropublisher. Realistically you're getting material that is too rough to get any traction with agents and the Big 5. You have to decide if it's a diamond in the rough. It's a judgement call. And the best of us get the wrong answer from time to time. If you say no, then the manuscript gets kicked back to the author; the author moves on and so do you.

But what if you make a qualified yes, a hesitant and negotiated yes?

What you should do is call the author and have a conversation. Tell them it needs to be scrubbed up and that can be a substantial amount of work and are they ready and willing for that to happen. You can have different versions of this spiel. They pay you for editing it; they pay someone else to edit it; you do it for free once the contract is signed. Each of these options has a down side. It might need to be more than one edit. Even if they pay you for the edit, it's no guarantee that it'll be accepted. You might not want to offer a contract until it's been professionally edited. Whichever route you choose to walk down, the work will need to be edited.

I can assure you of two things. The first is that they'll say there won't be any problems, none at all. The second is that there will be.

Let's say you decide to offer the author a contract and do all the editing in house. Then you give the manuscript (MS) to your intern to catch typos, repetition, strange plot devices, factual errors and egregiously bad grammar. The end result will be a document covered in red squiggles. *Wow*, thinks the author, *this is a whole lot better*. And indeed it is.

If you don't have an intern or you don't feel comfortable doing that yourself, then computer programmes might be able to do that for you. So far, the free samples that I've been asked to review, can't. But I'm pretty sure that AI will replace this kind of grunt editing soon.

The point is, the worst of the errors are gone and it'll be easier for you to go to work on it. And the author is thrilled at how it's already been improved. This establishes trust between you and the author.

Then you (or your interns) do a manuscript evaluation. This is good, this is bad, this works, this doesn't. You write a 7-10 page commentary about the manuscript, which you send to the author. You talk about it on the phone with them before you do the evaluation and afterwards.

ALWAYS ALWAYS ALWAYS be so nice that your own mother won't recognise you. Trowel on the praise. Slather it thick and deep. Your authors will not think that you're making it up or that you are taking the mickey. They'll think someone has finally recognised their value. Which you have.

Let's say you decide to help this author improve their work before you offer a contract. Whether you are a paid coach or do it for free is up to you. Encourage them to do things.

1. Join a writer's group or three. This is partially because they will get solid feedback but also because it gives them colleagues, a supportive friend group that is interested in the progress of the book and with whom they can share its journey.

2. Take a writer's course for exactly the same reason. The only difference is that writer's courses tend to be more competitive

to get into and everyone takes it much more seriously. But the feedback also tends to be much better, which *some* authors like.

3. Read how-to books. Goodness knows there are enough of them out there. No one ever does this, by the way, so your authors are going to ignore you when you suggest this. They think they're too good for how-to books, undoubtedly because you've spent considerable time telling them that they are utterly amazing. They'll think you're trying to get them to write to a template. What they don't get is that they haven't yet figured out the template, and why and how it works — and then became so comfortable with the rules that they tossed them out the window.

4. Tell them to read read read. As in a book a week, no exaggeration. Tell them to read with a pen in one hand, underlining phrases or paragraphs that work or might be of some assistance to their own work. If they're writing in a genre, then tell them to mostly read that genre. Tell them that they should have read at least 100 and ideally closer to 1,000 books in that genre, and have a good understanding of how they are put together, the strengths and weaknesses of the genre, who are the bestsellers and why. If your authors want to be professionally published, then it's fair enough to ask them to know their profession.

5. Offer tricks of the trade or exercises like:
    (a) Tell your authors to count the number of words that bestselling authors in their genre use to introduce a character, describe a setting or set up a plot. In other words, you can ask your authors to map out and dissect the first chapter, literally sentence by sentence, to get a feel for pacing and layout and plotting.

    (b) Get them to reduce their entire book to 50 words, 250 words, 750 words and 1,500 words. It's a very useful exercise.

    Hamlet, a prince, must decide whether or not his uncle and mother murdered his father, and if others he

trusts are in on it. If they're guilty, how then should he respond? Hamlet grapples with truth, justice and living with this knowledge. Meanwhile, a foreign country is invading. (48 words)

This is a pretty rubbish way to describe one of the greatest works of the English language. But it's an exercise in stripping away the non-essentials, not a love letter to Shakespeare. Do it again for Hamlet but this time adding in words. Get your authors to do it for multiple works that they are fond of, whether they are thrillers or non-fiction.

(c) J.K. Rowling recommends a spreadsheet of where everyone is at every time. This is especially useful if you're doing a thriller with overlapping timelines.

There are any number of exercises like this. Generally, though, you don't need to worry that your authors will do them endlessly. My experience has been that authors really fight doing them. They're writers because they like to write. They don't want to do spreadsheets and word counts and analyses of other people's books. As the editor, you have to encourage them to migrate from being a creator to being an analyst, from being a writer to an editor, from communing with the muse to communing with the craft. Because that's what we're talking about here. We're talking about learning the craft of writing.

Your job as a micropublisher is not to teach them how to write. Your job is to publish them once they've learned it. They have their job and you have yours.

Once the author gets the MS highly polished, they should be encouraged to share it extensively and get as much feedback as possible. So that would be with family and friends and neighbours, people on Facebook, absolute strangers. Anyone really who is interested in giving them feedback.

All this improves the calibre of the MS. The author learns how to self-analyse and rewrite. And you don't have to be the one giving them all these criticisms because everybody else already has.

Then the manuscript gets resubmitted to you. This is now where you have to decide: do you put a lot more work into this manuscript and publish it? Keep in mind, you've already spent an awful lot of time on this particular piece of work. Generally, for free. I have occasionally gotten a nice bottle of wine out of it for which I am grateful, but it's rarely more than that. And to be completely honest, if I come across a work that I've already professionally edited through Clapham Publishing Services – where I am a jobbing editor – I'm more inclined to take it. There's no guarantee of course, but getting paid somewhere along the line is like putting a thumb on the scales.

Let's say you decide to publish it. Phone them up and discuss individual words and what sounds better. Everyone loves doing that. You love it because you love words. The authors love it because it's about their work. And the reader loves it because the end result is miles better than when it started.

Now look, what I've just outlined for you is the ideal situation. It's the theory. In reality, steps can be missed or done out of order. I once spent three hours in front of a whiteboard helping an author sort out his characters and the plotting for his murder mystery. In theory, he should have done it by himself before it got to me. Sometimes life doesn't go that way.

Ultimately what I'm trying to say is that as a micropublisher, you have to work *with* your authors. You two are a team, even though each has their own role to play. Part of your job as the publisher is helping them do their job. But have boundaries. Be prepared to spell out your expectations. And be prepared to say no.

4D) What To Assess When You're Assessing

I'm all in favour of achievement. I'm rather fond of the feeling it brings: that glow of inner satisfaction that you hope doesn't translate into smugness – or at least not too much.

I assume everyone is in agreement with me on this one. Achieving is preferable to failing. Winning is more fun than losing. Success is better than defeat. Smugness beats depression.

Really, the only tricky bit is determining what counts as achievement and success and winning.

This section is about refereeing your emotions. How we understand what we are feeling, why we're feeling it and what we should do about it. This is rather a long discussion. I'm only going to introduce it because there's an entire career about refereeing your emotions called therapy. And I'm a publisher, not a therapist.

Nonetheless, here's goes.

TRUE STORY: I once had lunch with a senior editor from a hugely successful imprint of (let's say) HarperCollins. He was a nice man and I very enjoyed our lunch, which was on the sunny terrace of a major London museum. He'd been hired away from some other imprint and given a promotion. He was told that the new imprint was in the red and he had a year to turn it around. If he couldn't, then he'd be fired along with all the staff, and the imprint would be folded up with its backlist absorbed by other imprints. He was in his mid-40s, married, with small children and a mortgage. If he failed at this imprint, it would be unlikely that another publisher would hire him. So the stakes were high.

His first day on the job, he gathered round his editors and told them that they could only publish authors with a proven track record of making a profit. Every other author would be let go. Each editor got one and only one pet project. The editors baulked, saying that they were carrying many mid-ranking authors who might not be making money at this point but likely would be in the future. Editors pointed out that an author can make loads of money with one title and have the next one crash. Editors pointed out the numbers of gambles they'd taken with authors, which had paid off big time. That publishing was littered with authors who should have sold and didn't, and authors who shouldn't have sold and did. Publishing was as much a judgement and an investment as it was a spreadsheet.

My luncheon companion prevailed. Nothing that wasn't a guaranteed income earner was published. His imprint went into the black. He kept his job. He paid off his mortgage. He was celebrated. He was smug.

I'm not disagreeing with his decision. I'm just envious that it could be that simple: make money or else.

As a micropublisher and cancer survivor, I too have a definition of what constitutes success. I start with survival and good health. But that's the only simple part of the definition. The rest is complex, nuanced, negotiated and ever changing.

Initially, my definition of success for Claret Press was to just get some books out for authors so that they could say that they were published, and their books could enter the British National Library Catalogue (which self-published books cannot).

At a certain point I came, with considerable astonishment, to the realisation that I might live long enough to expect more from my publishing.

And that's when it became complicated. With the belief that ideas can enter into our subconscious and ultimately change our expectations and behaviours, and with considerable evidence that our liberal democracy is under threat, I wanted to create books that engaged with this reality yet were commercial, even fun.

As the red went redder, I realised I needed to be successful in other areas as well. I didn't have to make money, because that's an idiotic goal, but I did have to sell books. And that meant that I had to figure out accounting and margins, branding and marketing, social media and influencers.

So now I publish to protect and promote our democracies while finding other avenues to subsidise that endeavour. Which reminds me, this book would make a fabulous Christmas present for just about everyone on your list! Buy all the other Claret Press books as well. Or just give me money. I take donations in all currencies.

Joking aside, how do you judge success?

Here's my genuine and heartfelt belief: Success is more than totting up your sums and seeing if you're in the black while the threat of redundancy hangs over your staff and yourself. Success is about friendships and joy and learning. It's about acknowledging and valuing the things you can't see. It's about treating yourself as a whole person and your community as a gift. Success is about service and sharing and groping your way to all the kinds of riches that there can be. Otherwise, you're selling yourself short. And that's a terrible pity.

Part 5: ANNOUNCE

Celebrate your achievements – because they're worth celebrating! And share with the world that celebration – because it is worth sharing.

5A) Weighting the Dice

Let's first set out some qualifiers.

1. First, my little publishing company breaks even. I'm going to talk about strategies for breaking even, which is no mean feat. It's taken me the better part of a decade to break even. While this may sound ludicrous to you, I'm kind of proud of that. If you think that this chapter is going to tell you the secrets to making squillions, stop reading now and save yourself 20 minutes.

2. Here's my second qualifier. The world is not a fair place. There is no level playing field. The bigger you are, the easier it is to make money. As a micropublisher, you and I are at one extreme end of the spectrum: the toughest end to make any money at all. If your ambition is to make money from publishing, the best advice I can give you is to grow bigger and move along the spectrum from being a micropublisher to being a big publisher.

3. Third qualifier. There are so many jokes about how useless marketing is that it should make everyone squirm with discomfort. Here's probably the most famous: *50% of my marketing worked, I just don't know which 50%.*

4. My fourth qualifier. In a podcast in September 2023, *The Economist* magazine, drawing on figures from the USA and UK publishing market, stated that only 0.4% of titles cover their costs. Now, the sunk costs of a large publisher are more than for a small indie. So breaking even for the bigger publishers is selling 5,000+ copies a title. And less than half of 1% manage to do that. Very few titles carry the costs of publishing 99.6% of their products. Those of you who have a background in business will find that jaw-dropping to the point of being hard to believe.

In other words, no one has a clue.

Given that reality, how do we even understand marketing? I think of it as weighting the dice. Each book I publish has to make enough money that I don't go bankrupt. I can't do what the bigger companies do and find one massive international bestseller that will support publishing all my other books. So each title I produce has to wash its own face. But that's like rolling the dice and expecting nothing but double sixes.

Rolling double sixes each and every time is completely unreasonable — unless you weight the dice in favour of the side with the six dots. It is possible to roll the dice and not get double sixes. But on average and over time, you will roll more sixes than the odds predicted.

5B) Give to Get

People read because the experience gives meaning to their life. The meanings are diverse: the private pleasure of poetry, a sleeping aid, light entertainment while on a commute, a thrill, a romance to get the blood pumping, a history to learn and so on. Books provide meaning by creating a community around the shared experience of knowing the same character, living in the same artificial universe and resolving the same issue; the reader can talk about the book on various platforms and with real-world friends. Books provide meaning by explaining us to ourselves, like the world's cheapest therapist. Books provide meaning by validating and reinforcing, recognising and naming facets of ourselves. To misquote Bob Dylan, every book's got to serve someone.

By publishing, you are providing meaning to people. By publicising a book, you are making evident what people are actively seeking, and want so badly that they are willing to pay for it. You are making the world a better place by performing this important public service. Thank you.

When you realise that you are a service provider (like a nurse or a fireman) and not some grubby salesman, you can start to engage with marketing. It's why I wrote this book. I know things that people don't, and I want all of you to know these things too, so that we can create a world with more readers of better books from more effective micropublishers. Yes, I am selling it to you. But you wouldn't have bought it unless you really needed it. I am doing you the enormous favour of letting you have access to my knowledge for a modest fee. You're welcome.

The first thing you need to do is massage your understanding of marketing into a different shape altogether. What's the service you are offering? How are you helping people? What meaning are you creating? Why should anyone care about your books?

Once you have answered those questions, you have reshaped your understanding of marketing as a public service.

Let's say you publish dinosaur porn (yes, it really exists, I've interviewed the voice artist who read the audiobooks). Now that's a specialist interest that has undoubtedly been poorly served. By publishing dinosaur porn, you are making these people feel less lonely, less isolated. You are validating their desires. Bless your cotton socks for being so generous spirited. Not merely do you now have an understanding of what your publishing house offers and why, you have an understanding of what else you can do to help them: sell a blow-up T-Rex, promote discussions about asteroids and climate change, watch Jurassic Park on Discord. In effect, the marketing of dinosaur porn digresses from addressing the topic of getting undressed.

I'll share the meaning that underlies Claret Press, what I think it offers, what community I think it serves. This is a little personal so please bear with me.

Once, I was a freelance editor and a cancer-infused mom of kids aged 11, 13, and 15. At the time, the world was going to hell in a handbasket. The British had supported a political movement using (among other tactics) a drumbeat of racism and xenophobia, which many Brits demonstrated through the ballot box that they were pretty comfortable with by voting for Brexit. For the first time, I started being trolled on social media for being a foreigner, with people "screaming" at me to go home to Canada. Given that I am of Irish and Scottish stock, you could say I had already come home so it was more ludicrous than upsetting. Actually, it was hugely upsetting. That's why trolls do it. The Americans then did something almost as bad by electing Trump. If that wasn't enough, the world was literally on fire and/or being flooded because we have, over the decades, refused to make the changes necessary to ensure our own survival. We're losing our common sense, our common ground and our common future.

I was exiting this planet and leaving a worse world for my children to navigate. All I could do was apologise.

And then it seemed I was surviving. Oh. That was unexpected.

Quixotic it may be, but I decided to do something about our reality. Through storytelling, I am trying to improve our conversations with each other.

While providing an enjoyable read, my books share thoughts and experiences that deepen our understandings of our shared world. You can slide into a Claret Press book on the tube or in the tub, flipping pages happily. After all, you've had a long hard day, and you just want to relax with a great read.

Conversely you can analyse the same book as an insight into social, historical or political phenomena. The book's ideas could be part of a lecture or a Zoom. Even if you're more of a page-flipper than a Zoom-dipper, you absorb the ideas burbling in the background.

That's the meaning underlying Claret Press books: page-turners with background burbling. That's how I give service.

I sell to people who don't want to read a textbook on the problems of the world. On the other hand, they are curious, concerned and open-minded. To reach these people, I've hosted Zoom events and webinars with professors, union leaders, lawyers, former MPs, archivists and vicars. I have sometimes included my authors, my daughter and people from my community who have something to say. I have written blogs for a charity building a library in western Kenya. I have been interviewed on other people's podcasts. It's all wonderful fun and very humbling at the same time to be part of a larger debate on how to grapple with the challenges of our world. Admittedly, it hasn't sold many books … yet. But I do hope that somehow all the background burbling will initiate and consolidate actions that protect and promote our democracy.

5C) Look PRH. Feel PRH. Be PRH.

Packaging counts. You think publishing is all about the story or the quality of the writing or the value of the information that you're imparting. Yes, of course. And no.

Follow me as I go sideways to explain.

There is an old saying from before my time that was such an effective piece of advertising that it's been plucked from ad history and placed in a TV cop show as the sage advice the ageing cop dispenses to the rookie. The phrase is this: look sharp, feel sharp, be sharp.

It's from a 1952 ad campaign for Gillette razors. As a square-jawed hunk suggestively stroked the smooth mounds of his chin, the narrator intoned, *Look sharp. Feel sharp. Be sharp.*

What does all this have to do with micropublishing? It's this: your books have to look as if they're published by Penguin Random House. Your little micropress might be like my little micropress, and you're working from your kitchen table or the spare room of your house. But no one need know that.

Look PRH. Feel PRH. Be PRH.

This is especially true in the era of Instagram and TikTok, where the book cover and the images that can be made from the book cover are key to marketing your book.

So how do you make your books look PRH and feel PRH, so that you can **be** PRH? I'm going to give you a few tips.

The Cover Design
TRUE STORY: I was put in contact with a recently retired book sales rep. I invited her for a long leisurely lunch to talk books, publishing and of course the tricky business of selling. For a

sales rep, she was notably lacking in charm. She spent the lunch grumbling about the lousy weather and the state of her garden, asked me no questions about my little business and instead interrogated my intern about her love life. When I tried to redirect the conversation back to books, she told me that there was a reason why she'd retired.

After lunch, as I'm shooing her out the door as fast as possible, I waved a hand in the direction of my books, artfully displayed in my office. She marched over and, without a moment's hesitation, put her finger on each book that my designer had done. *That's a good cover*, she pronounced. And then named the publishing company that could have produced it. *Good*, she laid her finger on another book, *good, good, good*. Named more publishing companies. The rest, designed with the help of my authors or wholly by the authors, *meh*.

I was defensive (as I tend to be about my babies). *We work cooperatively with the authors to produce a cover that we all approve of, and many of the authors are themselves artistic and...*

She brushed it off with a disinterested shrug, zipped her coat up and left. Several days later, I received a very nice thank-you note and an invite for my intern to visit her.

I went back to my book display and examined it closely. The 100% accuracy of landing on the covers my designer had done. The total disregard for the covers which my authors and/or their friends had mostly designed.

It rather gave me pause for thought.

There are any number of videos on YouTube on how to create a good cover. As always, I recommend that you do your research and go to bookstores and check out what the professionals are producing. Here's the theory:

- Draw the eye in (translation: make it an arresting image)
- Put motion on the image (translation: the mind will turn an image into a video which is more engaging for the viewer if you

help the eye to do that, for example, put a picture of a windmill with trees being blown by the wind and the mind will automatically make windmill sails turn)
- Create tension (translation: making it an exciting image)
- Make it appropriate to thumbnail for easy sharing on social media (translation: make the image simple)
- Ensure that it is appropriate to the genre (translation: duh)

The inside design has to match the outside. There has to be the right amount of white space. If you're doing academic or textbooks or some non-fiction, you have wider borders than novels so that the reader can make notes. If your books are pleasure reads, then you have narrower borders – but not too narrow. It's still got to be easy to read. You don't want to cram as many words on the page as possible as that slows the eye down and makes the eye work harder to read.

I highly recommend getting a professional book designer. They'll know what kind of cover is appropriate for the genre you're producing and the amount of white space you need for margins for the genre you're producing, how to insert illustrations and how to create titles and how to organise chapters. It's more complicated than the talented amateur realises.

You can go on any number of platforms that sell services, such as Fiverr, Upwork or Reedsy. You can ask family and friends if they know of someone. I am happy to share the name of my own book designer if you email me (no strings attached).

If you do decide to go down that route of doing it yourself, keep in mind that there are plenty of free templates out there, free images and a ton of free tips and help and guidance on how to manipulate images, troubleshoot and create a good-looking book.

The interior of the book
I have met plenty of micropublishers who have taught themselves to create an excellent interior after taking a course on Adobe InDesign, the industry standard for creating a book.

It's a complicated programme to figure out, but once you've mastered it, if you need to make changes, you can just do it yourself rather than sending it away to the designer. It's not just cheaper, it's faster. There are advantages to you being the only person you need to rely on.

The only drawback to InDesign is that you have to buy a subscription to a whole suite of programmes and software that Adobe sells. It's too much. I just don't need the sheer complexity of the Creative Cloud suite and I don't need to share that subscription with nine other people who supposedly work in the office with me. A possible solution would be to find nine other micropublishers who need Adobe InDesign and share the cost with them. Instead I have a designer and she has InDesign.

Another option, which I've seen micropublishers do with some success, is printing every book from a professionally produced template or templates. I think that this is something they do in the business world where the quarterly reports always look like each other, and then the annual report looks the same but different. The end result looks just fine.

If you have to choose where to put your resources, put them into proofreading. There will still be typos. I promise you that. But you can reduce them. Here's how:

1. Get the author to get their friends to read the PDF and just look for typos. They'll want to comment on other things as well. Make sure that they are thanked in the acknowledgments – effusively.

2. Run your eye across the manuscript, looking for the blue/red squiggle that tells you there's a typo.

3. Get ProFormWriting or PerfectIt or one of those computer aids. They correct some typos. Use macros, if you can bear to learn how to use them.

4. Read it backwards from the last word on the last page. Do a minimum of 10 pages a day. On a good day, try to do 20.

5. Clean it up as you go along. So at every edit take out the typos as you see them.

If you use print-on-demand then you can produce a dozen or two dozen copies of the book and distribute them as ARCs (Advance Reading Copies) several months BEFORE the book actually goes on sale. The author gives them away as comps or shares them with book bloggers. The corrections dribble in. Then update the manuscript. Technically, I put stickies on the PDF and then send it back to the designer who updates it. And just before it's ready for publication, I upload the corrected version. So what the reader gets is as typo-free as is humanly possible.

Here are more tips for how to up your game on the interior:

Make sure that the stuff at the front of the book and the back of the book looks professional. The stuff at the front is called the front matter. And the stuff at the back of the book is called the end matter.

So you have professional-looking front matter with publishing information, a title page, a Table of Contents. At the back, you have a professional-looking end matter: About the Author, Acknowledgements, any additional information.

I'm always kind of surprised when micropublishers don't do this. It's low-hanging fruit, easy to pluck and ready to eat.

Here's a tip: Be careful not to overegg the pudding. Don't put a ludicrous amount of extra information in just because you can. It's the Goldilocks factor. You want to put in just the right amount.

The Size
Nowadays there is nothing standard about publishing. So if you want to do an idiosyncratic size, knock yourself out. Having said that, if you are trying to establish yourself as a Penguin Random House, then look at the sizes of their books and copy them. There is no need to reinvent the wheel here.

Like everything else, the genre indicates the size of the book. Pleasure reads like crime or romance tend to be smaller. Business books tend to be larger. If you're a bestseller, the size of your book grows. As Stephen

King went from being a writer of pulp fiction to a bestseller whose novels get analysed in EngLit, the actual physical size of his books grew – as did the number of words that he produced.

Beware of publishing books in A5. Bookshops can't put them on the shelves because they're taller than the other books. They can't be laid out neatly on a display table, again because they're a different size from all the other books and don't fit together well. So bookshops tend not to display them. People tend not to put them on their bookshelves and instead donate them to charity. I see something A5 now and think: *oooh must be self-published.*

5D) Digital

Subscribers

When it comes to marketing, you are not a micropublisher or a book lover or an author. You're fulfilling a service. You're doing your community a favour by supplying them with what they want. You're Mother Teresa. But even Mother Teresa had to find the people who needed what she had to offer. She moved from Albania to the slums of Calcutta, from teaching to ministering to the indigent. Similarly, you have to find the people who want your service.

The best way to do that is to create a subscriber community of those who want what you're offering. You tell them when it's available. You offer them deals and unique insights. You keep them abreast with what's going on. In theory this keeps your community engaged with what you are offering. In return, you get solid feedback: which books are selling, which aren't; what topics are people emailing you about; what else your community needs from you.

Apparently, about 5% of subscribers engage with newsletters. This is considered to be AMAZING because Twitter gets something like 0.1%. Or was it 0.001%? To my way of thinking, it doesn't matter so much because when the numbers get that low, it becomes irrelevant.

Subscriptions are usually done by gathering email addresses. The obvious question is, how do you go about getting everyone's email address?

Here's another joke about marketing:

> Knock knock
> Who's there?
> A free ebook
> A free ebook who?
> Just fill in your email address and this 14-line form of personal info and... hello? hello? ... ... Knock knock

Ask readers to subscribe on the last page of your books. Perhaps you go to book festivals or summer fairs and there you talk to people about your books. Perhaps you organise fundraisers or a competition or a zoom webinar or do voluntary work. Have everything already lined up: a good-looking website, a QR code for people, a leaflet of your publications, explicit exhortations to subscribe. Which reminds me, subscribe to Claret Press for our latest news and events and special deals.

Basically, it's brutally hard work to get those subscribers. It's not always fun and I can't say that I always enjoy the experience. But that's just me. Perhaps you'll have a blast. I hope you do.

Once people subscribe, you foster the connection:

1. Send out a newsletter once a week or once a month or whenever. I have heard that it's supposed to be absolutely regular, but I can't make that happen. I send out a newsletter when I have both the time and the news. This is about once a month. In the summertime, never. Over Christmas, also never. No one has ever once complained about the newsletter being irregular or non-existent.

2. In that newsletter, make sure you have embedded links to any books you are selling or events you are organising. Don't make it difficult for your subscribers to order the books that you are selling.

3. Keep the newsletter short. Save your writing for your books.

4. Include photos. I have two pets, one an adorable dog and the other a killer kitty. They regularly make the newsletter. I also include pictures of book launches, authors, London Book Fair, book cover reveals.

5. Have a sale every month for one reason or another. Then your readers will open up the newsletter every month just to see what's on sale.

6. I include a link to an occasional blog posting that I wrote.

7. Include a small extract from the book you are publishing. It's a hook.

8. Create a SurveyMonkey Q&A for your subscribers to click on to give you feedback, with no more than six questions in it and a space for them to add on anything extra that they feel like sharing. I would think that this could be occasional, but I always encourage people to give me feedback regardless at the Claret Press contact email address.

Social Media

TRUE STORY: While sharing a pizza and a beer with a former intern, now a director of marketing at a mid-sized British publisher, I asked her, "Does social media work, because I don't seem to be selling any books from it." She chose her words carefully. "It does if it's done correctly."

The uncomfortable conclusion was that I was not doing social media properly, and neither were Claret Press authors.

What counts as correctly? If it is done correctly, you get a huge number of followers and sell books to them. If you don't have a huge number of followers and people don't buy your books, then I am afraid to say that you are not doing it right. Near as I can determine, almost no one does it right. Even doing it "not-wholly-badly" is sufficiently unusual that it counts as a win. As the saying goes, in the land of the blind, the one-eyed man is king.

Here's the theory:
Many micropublishers use social media to get subscribers, to whom they then sell their books. So you make your social media so utterly fabulous that people subscribe so as not to miss a post.

But people can follow you on social media who don't necessarily care that much one way or another. They're just charmed by your posts. Confusingly, you can then have high numbers of followers and still not sell a book. Or at least not sell enough to justify the blood, sweat and tears you put into your posts.

Really work at least one social media platform and make that your digital presence. A social media platform can best be understood as a Swiss Army knife. Most people use just the blade to cut things. But there are all the other attachments: the corkscrew and the screwdriver and the scissors and even the saw. Social media is the same. The more you work one social media platform, explore it and push it and see what works, the more you try things out and check the response, the more useful it becomes until it's a very handy tool. In other words, don't just post.

Remember that social media is social. That is, liking and commenting on others' posts is more important than posting your own. Behave on social media as you would at a dinner party: enquire how people are, admire their children's achievements, praise the food, tell a witty story, share a titbit. Using social media is exhausting because it's like being the only well-mannered guest at an all-you-can-eat pig-out.

I will say this about social media. When I started out everyone had to be on Facebook, get a Facebook business page, promote on Facebook. You were nothing without Facebook.

Then it became Twitter. Then LinkedIn. Then Instagram. Now it's TikTok. My son, the engineer, wants me to go on Reddit. By the time you read this, some other social media will be invented, and I can guarantee you that it'll be the "must use" one.

The real issue is: Can you get any social media platform to actually work for you? That is, can you connect with your readers, build your subscription list and sell your titles using social media? If you can't figure out how to use one, then I don't know why you would bother switching to a new platform. But if you have had a degree of success with (let's say) Facebook, then you might expand to another platform.

If you don't do social media, well, that just means that you have to find other ways to make a noise.

5E) Tried and True

I can hear what you're saying: what about contacting the local radio station, the local TV station, getting a book review in the newspaper? After all, that's where you get your recommendations: Book at Bedtime on Radio 4.

Sure. Send them a copy of the book and the AIS (Advance Information Sheet). If you have a string to pull, then I would recommend pulling it.

Good luck with that one.

AIS or Press Release

There is a device which has changed little over the decades in publishing. It's called an Advance Information Sheet (AIS). The AIS is made pretty much as soon as you've signed the contract with the author. It's one page of information that allows someone to learn everything they need to know about that book just by running their eye across the page. This information includes the following:

- ISBN for both paper and ebook (if hardcover, include that. For that matter include all formats and all ISBNs)
- Size of the book (its dimensions and its number of pages)
- Price
- Where and how it's available (for example, my distributor in the UK and EU is Gazelle and my distributor in the rest of the world is IngramSpark print-on-demand)
- What its target audience is (that is, children ages 9-12, women's book clubs)
- Keywords (political thriller, cosy mystery, vampire romance, history of trains and railroads)
- Publication date

This information is usually presented as bullet points.

The AIS is also a honey trap. There are endorsements, a hook, awards, a catchy blurb, a picture of the gorgeous cover, a picture of the author with 25 words about them, all artfully displayed as a visual feast. It's a mix of the prosaic and the seductive.

It's really very useful once you have created it. You can use it as a press release. You can send it to bookshops that you think might be interested in it. You can share it through your monthly newsletter. You can press it into the hands of agents who might be interested in representing your books. There it all is, in a nutshell. When you're at those fairs and book fests, it can sit at the edge of the table for anyone who walks by.

A press release is the same but different. It is generally two pages. Take out the stuff that really only interests people in the book trade (size, keywords, target audience), and increase the information like stats that show why the book is relevant to today's market, a paragraph extraction, slogans. Include information about the author, such as their availability for media interviews.

I have been known to create a two-page press release, especially with non-fiction, with the second page being a 750-1,000 word synopsis of the book itself, with all the key data and links to relevant websites which augment the information. In effect, you've done all the work for the journalist who now doesn't have to read the book or do any research. This is especially if you want your local newspaper to cover it.

Books in Series
Here's another joke: How do you sell your first book? You publish your seventh.

LOL. ROFL. Insert appropriate emoji here along with other acronyms.

Ideally, people get hooked on your characters. So you want to publish a series. Crime and romance, fantasy and self-help, these genres effortlessly produce books in series. I have seen business books in a series, plus biographies, histories, memoirs, cookbooks, gardening, historical fiction, adventure fiction and so on. If you think strategically, then anything can be turned into a series.

I'm not cut from that bolt of cloth. I find the idea of producing a series overwhelming. When an author happily confides that they've got another six books sitting in the bottom drawer, it feels like a tsunami of words. *Six,* I'll murmur, *goodness.*

And that's probably another reason why I don't sell as many books as I should.

Face-to-Face
My experience suggests that nothing sells like face-to-face and nothing sells like a personal recommendation. Personal beats impersonal. The facts back me up. So go out and meet people.

This is what I tell my authors to do (although not all of them):

1. Have multiple book launches with different groupings. Make them small and more intimate. Here's why: they're just more fun. People are more likely to walk away with a smile on their face and feel positively inclined towards your book and as a result, recommend it on.

   Hit every book club you can: the local library's, your friends', your neighbours', the Women's Institute, online book clubs. Your extended family should hold launches for you. Your mother lives in one part of the country, your brother in another, your favourite cousin and a flatmate from your profligate youth in two other. Time to go on a road trip and visit them with a box of books in the backseat of the car. Take plenty of wine, cheese and crackers. Have a little (less than 5 min) talk prepared in which you are witty and caring, informed and insightful. Read a page (less than 3 min). Have your daughter sing a song or recite a poem that relates to your book. If she has a good voice, get her to sing a second song or recite more. Play a short video (less than 5 min). Take questions from the floor (less than 5 min).

TRUE STORY: A friend went to a book launch of a mutual friend. He'd invited everyone he knew to it. Turned out he knew a lot of people. My friend said to me, outraged: *He invited us just to get us to buy his book.* I clucked sympathetically but thought: Is there any other reason to invite people to a book launch?

What you want to do is create a personal connection with your readers and you offer some entertainment. Then you rinse and repeat as you work your way across the country.

Ideally, you'll have already created your website, and so have your authors. You have brought with you the leaflets that summarise your books with a QR code to websites: yours, Amazon's, the indie bookshop's. So if they didn't bring money or they want to wait a month until their next paycheque, it's still very easy for them to buy it.

2. Create larger events in which the author is a participant. One of my authors, frustrated that she couldn't get into her local book festival, created an alternate book festival and then gave herself the best table and the best speaking slots, which seemed fair enough to me.

   Another author, who is very political, creates platforms with herself and local MPs and other political activists to discuss issues which reflect (slightly) the issues in her book. Bookshops aren't that interested, but other groups are, and she talks to them.

   Another author created events where she and two other authors (whom I had not published) all spoke on the same topic of female detectives. They took it on the road and the three of them sold to each other's fans and found new ones as well.

3. Think outside the box. If you publish murder mysteries, then organise a murder mystery night. Or bring in a specialist to organise it and sell tickets. It doesn't have to be based on any of your books. Do the same if you publish romance only, make it about love, not death. If you publish books in which your characters walk a lot (think of Jane Austen's books where the dashing hero and witty heroine are always bumping into each other as they

tramp across a field), or if you live in a specific town, then organise a walking tour. Start with what you publish on and then think what your readers would be interested in. Vampires? Then cemeteries. Adventure on the high sea? Then a sailboat tour.

4. There many small local street fairs, church sales, foodie events, craft sales for Christmas, street celebrations, book fests, poetry readings, writing cooperatives. One of my better-selling authors wiggles his way into every single one that he possibly can. He helps to set up and take down tents and does a coffee run. He promotes the events on his twitter account. He is a real asset and gets invited back year after year. I think he rather enjoys them. He makes friends doing this as he otherwise spends a lot of time alone with his computer. So he considers this a bonus. Keep in mind that he can collect subscribers at these events and charge whatever he wants for his books to recoup the cost.

5. Meet the local librarians of as many libraries as you possibly can. Tell them you would be happy to organise a workshop on writing a memoir (if you publish memoirs), an analysis of Agatha Christie (if you publish murder mystery), give a talk on a foreign country (if you publish travelogues). Libraries won't want to do it because it's extra work for librarians and they are already overworked and underpaid as is. So volunteer to show up with posters that they can put up, put out the chairs and promote it through your own social media because libraries are desperate to get bums on seats. In other words, make this all gain and no pain for the libraries and you might be in. Then onto the next library.

6. Organise more or less the same thing for bookshops. Again, make this all gain and no pain for the bookshops because they also want bums on seats.

You can see from all of this that you have to initiate contact and from that, sell your books yourself. If you're like me, this sounds like a fate worse than death. I have learned to start small and hope no one shows up. Sometimes people do, which is distressing.

I keep going back to this statement so apologies if I sound repetitive: Who is reading your books? And why? How are they finding your books? That's your first step. The second is to do all the little mechanical things that I have outlined in this chapter: appropriate design, good website with subscribers, social media, face-to-faces, endorsements, press releases, initiating contact, innovative approaches.

If you find this a little daunting, you are a smart person because it really is daunting. Take a deep breath.

Part 6: ADVANCE

Congratulations! You are now a publisher. It might be of your own books and your friends'. It might be as the marketing arm of another business. You might be publishing total strangers. It doesn't matter. You have now chosen, produced and distributed for sale the creative output of a writer.
It's no small achievement. You might want to stop there. Draw a deep breath and think to yourself: I'm done now.
This is enough.

But you might want to take another step.
You're in the learning zone.
If you've gotten this far, you don't see why you can't go further. Then this chapter is for you.

6A) How to Get the Most out of IngramSpark

I've been using IngramSpark for about eight years to publish a good couple dozen books. This means that I can share some solid tips on how to really work it. I'm talking about school of hard knocks advice, the stuff that I had to learn the hard way.

1. Upload your books months in advance. And I do mean months. Partially, this is so all the metadata can go through the system before the book is published. But mostly, it's to get pre-orders on Amazon, which kick-starts the whole demand-driven machinery. Amazon, Waterstones and Barnes & Noble list books based on the demand for them. If, on the day the book is published, half a dozen copies are already bought, then that's the grease that moves the wheels. This also means that you can do pre-publication publicity and you can direct everyone to pre-order the books. In addition, there are book bloggers who won't review your book unless it's already up on Amazon, available for pre-order.

   Similarly, get the mates of the author to order the book through their local bookshop, Waterstones, Barnes & Noble, Amazon, whatever. This is instead of holding a launch party and having everyone buy it directly from the author. (Still have the party, of course, because you really need to celebrate what you have achieved.)

   Buying the book stimulates the demand algorithm. Amazon might say it's unavailable to order. Order it anyway. Tell the author to order a copy or two from Amazon and Waterstones soon after it's been released, say in the first few weeks. Again, it's the grease that moves the wheels of your distribution. It means that at your book launch party, everyone will already have a copy so you won't sell that many. But it also means that the digital world has registered your book's existence.

TRUE STORY: I was once at a book launch where there were no books for sale. Instead, the author had his kids wandering around with laptops and iPads, so that people could order it right there from Amazon and Waterstones and Bookshop.org. I was a little taken aback but could see the logic of it.

2. Use up all the metadata that you possibly can. IngramSpark will only send a little to Amazon. But what it does send is the BIG DESCRIPTION and it's flipping huge. So you can put into it all sort of other things besides the book description.

In the big description, start off with any endorsements:

THIS IS AN AMAZING READ, by a big-name celebrity.
ANOTHER AMAZING ENDORSEMENT, by someone else.

Followed by you writing: 90% 4 or 5* reviews on Amazon and Goodreads.

Make sure that the wording looks right with the spacing and the titles in italics. Once you've gotten it as good as you can make it, wait a few days for it to churn through the system and then you check it out on Amazon. Does it look right? Could it look better? If there's room for improvement, go back to IngramSpark and tweak it. Then wait a few days. Check it out on Amazon again. And tweak it again on IngramSpark. You should be regularly and immediately updating your metadata on IngramSpark all the time. You don't just input the information once and walk away. This is an ongoing cultivation, like a garden.

3. After the endorsements, put in the grab or the hook.
GODZILLA MEETS KING KONG. IT'S A MONSTER OF A LOVE STORY.

Then a space, and then the long description. Don't worry if there's some repetition. I mean, it's not ideal but it's not a deal breaker either.

The longer you can keep them reading **about** the book, the more likely it is that they'll buy the book. And that is the point of it all.

4. A good way to reduce your costs is to do a bulk order. A qualifier: the order will have to be sent to one address. Let's say you have several authors who live in or around Oxford and one who lives in Scotland but has a kid at school near Oxford. Get all the orders sent to Oxford and use it as a hub. Then you disperse the books to your authors.

   Here's why: IngramSpark has a handling fee for every order you put in. Let's say you order one copy of a title. The handling fee is £1.65 (at the time of writing). If you order 150 copies of one title, the handling fee jumps up to £4.50. Personally, I think that this is gouging and IngramSpark ought to be ashamed of itself, but they haven't asked me my opinion. Now if you add onto those 150 copies of one title, a single test copy of a different title, 10 copies of a third title from a different author and two copies of a fourth title, then guess what the handling fee is? It's still £4.50.

   Despite the increase in the number of books, the package and postage doesn't seem to go up commensurately. It's like books are being mailed to you for free.

   This is why you lump all these micro-orders together.

5. Upload the cover first. IngramSpark checks the cover in New York, and it'll take days. In comparison, the EPUB and the interior PDF are checked by a computer and it takes a few minutes. So if you are pressed for time and you've got to hit a deadline, then do the cover first. While New York is checking it out, you have a few days to get the final PDF interior and EPUB up. It's a tiny amount of breathing room but if you need that, then prioritise the cover.

6. If something goes wrong, and goodness know that happens to the best of us, immediately email them. You might wait 7-10

days to hear back from them. If you've got that much time, then sure, wait it out. My experience has been that if there's a problem, then you've got to fix it immediately. You don't have 7-10 days. This is a glitch in the IngramSpark service provision. I've been known to phone the USA when the lines here in London are closed. I've been known to email them, then do a chat discussion on the same issue, then email them again. Be the squeaky wheel. Make some noise. They won't love you for it, but your problem will be addressed and resolved quicker, if only to get you off their backs. I'm sure that they've got a bullseye somewhere in their office with a picture of me on it. I don't care. Throw darts at me until you give yourself repetitive strain injury. Just solve my problem now.

7. If you need to cancel a title for whatever reason, and I have cancelled several, then you have to email them. They don't like cancelling titles. I don't know why not. Send IngramSpark an email. Don't mess about pressing buttons, trying to figure out how to do this yourself. Because then what happens is that — if you're like me — you'll screw everything up by pressing the wrong button and that'll have to be sorted before they can cancel the title. It just gets messy. So simply email them.

All of these tricks and secrets I can personally say worked for me. It's these tiny little hacks across systems that slightly raise your game. And those slight gains can add up to a big difference.

6B) Agents, Scouts and Selling Your Rights On

You publish some great books that don't get the traction that they should because you're a micropress. But that's ok because you can sell the translation rights or the right to republish in English in other markets VIA AN AGENT OR A SCOUT, and it becomes a form of passive income.

And you think to yourself: Whoo-hoo! That's what I'll do. I'll find the diamonds in the rough, polish them up until they gleam in the sunlight and get praiseworthy reviews and/or endorsements so that everyone knows what a great read it is because I'm an award-winning editor. Then I'll inform agents and scouts. They'll want my books because it's easier for them for three huge reasons:

1. There's no editing involved so no investment of time and money in labour costs

2. There's no seeking out of new authors with all those risks: it's time consuming, the author could turn out to be a jerk or the author could be a one-hit wonder

3. There's no agent to pay because micropresses are very affordable compared to anything that has to do with agents

So the cost and the risk to capital are minimal. This is a win-win. Win for me because my authors then go up the ladder to the big boys. Win for the big boys because they've haven't risked their capital on an expensive award-winning editor; I've already done the work for free.

It's so persuasive logically that I'm taken aback that it doesn't actually happen. Big publishers, agents and scouts are not combing through micropresses to cherry-pick their authors. And I really couldn't tell you why not. This doesn't mean that as a micropress you can't sell on your rights, but that it's unlikely.

Before I go further, I'm going to lay out some terminology.

An agent represents authors and sells their work to a publisher. But equally, an agent can represent an entire publishing company and sell on their works to a foreign publisher. The micropress acts like an author, with an agent to represent it. That agent can sell books in a foreign language or sell in English to a different market.

As a micropress or small indie, you can find these agents and ask them to represent you. They might say yes. But also, these agents might approach you and ask to represent your books. Well sure, you say, knock yourself out.

I've had more of these agents reach out to me than I can shake a stick at. And then I never hear from them again. They might have literally thousands of books a year to sell on their rights and my little micropress is just one of hundreds of small indies that they're representing. After a while, the silence is resounding. So I email them and, like authors, don't even get the courtesy of a response.

I'm somewhat philosophical about it. These agents are easy for me to get. They approach me after every book fair. We exchange complimentary emails for several weeks. I email my AIS and press release and sometimes even copies of the books. And then it's all over. It's like a flirtation that never extends past exchanging phone numbers.

In my opinion the reason why the agents can't sell on my books is because I can't sell enough of them here in England. Nothing succeeds like success. If my books don't sell well in my own market, then there's no reason to think that another publishing house in a foreign market will fare any better. Because an agent makes their money as a % of the RRP of each copy sold, they're not going to risk their time and energy and contacts and goodwill selling on something that doesn't look as if it'll earn anybody any money.

Now, what's a scout?

A scout is like an agent but it cherry-picks from the publisher. It goes from publisher to publisher. There aren't as many scouts as there are agents. They don't deal with authors. They can sometimes work for just one publisher. They scan the works of other publishers, meaning micropresses, for books that would suit their bosses. Or they can be independent. Like agents, they specialise. Like agents, they need to pick winners because they get paid a % of every copy sold. And like agents, my success with them has been zip, zero, nada, nothing.

So I have to admit, I don't bother anymore. Why would I? If I ever managed to figure out how to flog a book to anyone ever, I'd get interested in this again. Otherwise, I haven't got the time to waste.

Having said that, I have in fact sold books in translation, and sold on the global rights to three of my books, and turned down an offer for a fourth. Let's just deal with the money first because it's the easiest. If this is to supply me with a passive income, well, it's not much of an income. But a little bit of something is better than nothing at all. So I'm not complaining. It's just much less than I had planned on it being. It's much less than the internet promised me that I'd make.

Now let's deal with how to go about doing it. You have to deal micropress to micropress. Skip the scouts. Skip the agents. Skip the big boys in publishing. Find your partners yourself. This is a great job for interns or yourself on a night when there's nothing else to do. Go through micropresses looking for ones that are like you. They publish the kind of books you publish but in French or Spanish or German.

Let's say you publish on the park benches of South London. Find the French micropress that sells books about street benches on the Champs Elysée. And a German micropress that publishes on park benches of Tier Garten in Berlin. And so on. You can methodically go through the Frankfurt Book Fair directory or just surf the web.

To sell the rights to *Brushstrokes in Time* by Sylvia Vetta, I had an intern who methodically went through every single publishing house registered with Frankfurt Book Fair, looking for a press that published books about China. She found one and emailed it. Drachenhaus Verlag is a micropress like Claret Press, and the owner told me that she'd been looking for a while for a novel that told the story of post-Mao China. She was tickled pink that we'd found her. And we were tickled pink that she said yes immediately.

In comparison, when I sold the global rights to Sarah Gray's trilogy, it was because a micropress in the USA found us through the Frankfurt Book Fair. Again, they were tickled pink and so was I.

Micropress to micropress means that they don't have to pay an agent. None of us sell well. That's why we're micros. So we're not expecting large sales from each other. It's about filling a hole in each other's publishing brand. It's about not having to spend time and money editing and proofreading a work. It's about sharing marketing images and copy so that all can prosper.

It's labour-intensive and haphazard — but what isn't? More to the point, it's the only way that I've been able to figure out how to sell rights abroad.

6C) Hacks that Help you Advance

These are simple things that I think are the basics. Anyone can do them, even me.

First. Design. Get a professional-looking website. And by that, I mean: copy one. You don't need to reinvent the wheel. You don't need to be original. That's what your books are there for. Instead, you need to be professional. So copy the professionals. Choose a publisher that is so big it has a professional website. And then copy it.

Let's say you publish fantasy. Copy the website of Gollancz. Or you publish romance. Copy Avon Books.

You should have a design element that is consistent, not just on the website but across the board. This includes a professionally produced logo. Get a colour scheme. Get your logo in a range of colours and styles, black on a white background, white on a black, as a banner, with and without words. And then make sure that the colour scheme gets carried across the website and social media so that you're consistent. This is less true for things like font, but it is true for the logo and the colours.

Carry that design professionalism through the covers. And again, the interior of the books has to be designed to look professional. There's a high cost if you fail on that one.

And by the way, people won't notice if you get the website and the design elements right. They'll only notice if you get it wrong. Because if it looks right, it's professional and therefore it is invisible.

My designer (who created the logo for Claret Press and who has done any number of my covers) is available on a freelance basis. I'm happy to share her contact details with you.

Second. Editing. If you possibly can, put a lot of effort into making sure that your books don't have typos or character's name change halfway through. It's those kinds of details that drive people ratty. They don't mind plot holes so big that you can drive a lorry through them. But man oh man, a typo is treated like a car crash.

My proofreader also works on a freelance basis. I'm happy to share her contact details with you.

Third. Awards. Now look, everyone likes awards. Who doesn't like an award? But there are awards and then there are awards. There are awards that no one has heard of and the kind that everyone has heard of. The first doesn't really help you so much. The second makes all the difference in the world.

Here's an ugly little truth about awards. There's a zillion of them. And 99% of them — the ones no one has heard of — are revenue earners for the people who run them. That is, you pony up your cash and then you get shortlisted or an honourable mention. You and everyone else. Then you buy a whole bunch of stickers from the award company which you slap on the cover of your book. The average reader doesn't know this and thinks it's amazing; they're reading a shortlisted winner.

Because readers don't know the difference, you might think that you might as well do it. But I can't recommend it. Authors find it humiliating. They don't want to buy their way into being shortlisted. And when someone does find out, it demeans both you and your books. Winning those kinds of awards doesn't strengthen your publishing house, not in the long run. Once I realised this, I stopped applying for those awards.

Instead, I apply for the big awards. Occasionally, Claret Press books get longlisted or shortlisted. Technically, what makes the biggest difference is getting on the shortlist. That gets you the biggest jump in readers, not winning. To date, I'm always the bridesmaid and never the bride.

What I do for awards is create an Excel spreadsheet (or Google Sheets or a table from Microsoft Word) and input a lot of information about the awards that are reasonable for Claret Press to apply for. The table includes key pieces of information about the kind of books the award committee is looking for, the website, the cost, the number of copies the committee wants and in which format, the approximate date it needs to be submitted by and any other little titbit of info I glean.

Once a month (that is, about as often as I update my metadata) I run my eye across it and see what's on for that month. Then I see if it's worth submitting a book for anything. This might take as long as 10 minutes. Mostly it takes no time at all. So this is not a time suck. But if you look at my website, the top banner, the first thing you see, is all the awards we've been shortlisted for. It looks pretty impressive. It's not wholly because my books are better than anyone else's – although they are – but because I have applied and applied and applied. Appropriately. Punctually. Paid in full. It's a steady rain that soaks.

Fourth. Catalogue and celebrate everything. You're going to London Book Fair. Hoorah Hurrah! No one need know that absolutely everyone is let in once they've paid the entrance fee. Got a cover design? Announce it. Got your author speaking on some Zoom event? Announce it. Got a book launch? Announce it.

You trumpet this stuff like a town crier. Loud. Repetitive. Professional.

And people think: *gosh but that's a striving and busy little publishing company. Damn right*, you think, *I am that amazing.*

Fifth. Get endorsements. If you want to make your books sell better and your publishing house look more sophisticated, get endorsements from important people. I do genuinely ask my friends to ask their friends to get a personal contact with these people, but I must have the worst network in the world because, hand on heart, we know no one. Sometimes I (or the author) cold call VIPs. The majority say no (the bastards). But a tiny minority say, *Yes, send me the manuscript and I'll read and comment.* (May a thousand blessings rain on their houses and their heirs). And that tiny minority makes all the difference in the world to micros like us.

6D) How to Punch Above Your Weight

Not everyone wants to be published by a tiny little publisher run by a middle-aged lady, tapping away at her computer in her PJs. People think that Claret Press is bigger than it is — and I don't disabuse them of that idea.

Let me tell you how I did it so that you can too.

If I had to reduce it to one word, that word would be consistency — across all fields. As a micropublisher you do about 20 things in any single day: accounting, marketing, editing, metadata, uploading, talking to authors, checking distribution, etc.

Take a long hard look at your little micropress. You know you're doing something amazing but equally, nobody's perfect. We've all got strengths and weaknesses. You need to channel your inner critic, the one your therapist tells you not to listen to. She tells me, *You're weak in this area*. Now I know what I've got to improve.

Then you turn your attention to the second weakest area. And you strengthen it. Once you get absolutely all the components and actions that you do at the same consistent level, you raise the level.

Easy to say. Hard to do.

Even though I have a very helpful inner critic, I struggle to get clarity about what I'm good at and what I'm not. So I've developed the Three-Legged Stool analysis.

Stools are amazing little pieces of furniture. Hilariously simple, surprisingly versatile and insanely strong. Stools impress the hell out of me. If there is reincarnation, I want to come back as a three-legged stool.

But make one leg too short, even by a little, and it's useless.

Apply the Three-Legged Stool analysis to your micropress.

Break your micropress into three areas, and by that, I mean the whole project.

I made the three legs of the Claret Press stool (you can choose other areas):

1. Production of the book
2. Marketing (selling) the book
3. Money

Let's look at just book production. Production's three legs are:

1. Choosing the MS
2. Editing
3. Designing

Let's break the editing down into its three legs:

1. Deep edit
2. Line edit
3. Proofread

Break the deep edit into its three legs:

1. The deep edit
2. The discussion with the author about it
3. The rewrite

And so on. Each three-legged stool has a three-legged stool inside it, like fractals.

Go as far as you can until you really can't break it down anymore. That's where you start. This is where you have to be honest with yourself. How good are you at the three parts of this smallest fractal of this stool? And what constitutes good?

You've a good grasp of your own strengths and weaknesses. Life has taught you that. So trust yourself to evaluate how you yourself are. If you think that you're good, then you are that good. Whoo-hoo. Pat yourself on the back.

The whole point of these three-legged stools is to have a private conversation with yourself. You become your own business mentor. Where are you the weakest? What do you need to work on the most? What is the core problem and why do you have it? And critically: Are you prepared to overcome your own weaknesses?

It requires a level of honesty and introspection that most of us dodge. I'm very truthful to others, if only because I'm a terrible liar. But I lie brilliantly to myself. So this discussion will not generate easy answers. Sorry about that.

You do not get to not answer the questions. You don't get to answer them badly. No lying. No cheating. No half-truths. You grope your way to some kind of insight until you've turned over all the stones in your psyche and looked underneath. And once that has happened, you work on those weak bits until they're no longer weak. You enhance and strengthen them until they're just as strong as all the other links.

And then you go up a level of the three-legged stool, expanding out.

My core problem was (and remains) marketing. It wasn't until I reconfigured marketing as a public service that I was able to engage with it. It stopped being about me and started being about you. And it is absolutely why I wrote this book: to help others.

But it took me a long time to arrive at that.

I want to assure you that you will get tremendous satisfaction from learning new skills, acquiring greater understanding of yourself and watching your company grow. I'll get together with my friends over a cup of coffee or a glass of wine (a fine claret), and they'll grumble about their exhausting jobs and their demanding bosses and their useless colleagues, and I'll have to stay silent because doing this feels great, really fabulous. It feels good enough to be illegal.

So don't be afraid to figure out your weaknesses. No one needs to know about them but you. This is between you and your stools.

Finally

Just before I sent it off to be proofread, I read over this manuscript. The sheer volume of information kind of overwhelmed me. I swear it looks trickier than it is. You start at the beginning and take the first step. Then you make yourself a cup of hot chocolate and read a book because you're done for the day. The next day you take another step. Another hot chocolate. Another book. Give it six months and you'll be astonished at how far you've travelled and how much you've learned. Step by step. Hot chocolate by hot chocolate. It worked for me.

Having said that, I didn't build this little micro press all by myself. Far from it. I'd like to thank from the bottom of my heart:

> the authors who entrusted their manuscripts to me, many of whom have become my good friends, a gift for which I am grateful;
>
> Petya Tsankova, the world's best book designer, and Frances Stormer, the world's best proofreader;
>
> my mother, who lent me seed money to start up Claret Press for no good reason that I could think of;
>
> my brother and sister, who patiently walked me through the basics of doing business and shared their considerable knowledge;
>
> my gorgeous and wonderful kidlets, who have helped me in ways big and small;
>
> my friends Carrie, Judy, Dianne, Karen, Mary Lucille, but especially Sarah and Philippa, who patiently endure me droning endlessly on until they want to stick fingers in their ears and hum merrily;
>
> the interns who have given me far more than I could ever have given back;
>
> and finally, to the best and most supportive and loving man in the world, with kisses.

To those who publish books, I salute you and wish you the very best.

www.ingramcontent.com/pod-product-compliance
Lightning Source LLC
Chambersburg PA
CBHW030301100526
44590CB00012B/474